The Wanderings of a Mountain Fly Fisher

The Wanderings
of a
Mountain Fly Fisher

TALES FROM A CATSKILL EDDY
AND OTHER TROUT WATERS

Ed Ostapczuk

Epigraph Books
Rhinebeck, New York

Paperback ISBN: 978-1-954744-68-4
eBook ISBN: 978-1-954744-69-1

Library of Congress Control Number: 2022905137

Cover watercolor by Lois Ostapczuk
Book and cover design by Colin Rolfe

Epigraph Books
22 East Market Street, Suite 304
Rhinebeck, NY 12572
(845) 876-4861
epigraphps.com

This volume is dedicated to the memory of Edmund William Sens, a Neversink fly fisher and creative fly tyer ahead of his time, perhaps forgotten by some, but not so for this author.

Acknowledgments

Regarding the work contained within on Ed Sens, to whom this book is dedicated, I owe a debt of thanks to the late Roger Menard for inspiring me down a path of discovery.[1] I also want to thank Wade Burkhart, who, like Roger, was a member of the Catskill Fly Tyers Guild and able to confirm some of the research that I couldn't. And I want to thank Pat Wellington of the Neversink Association and Carol Smythe of Time and the Valleys Museum in Grahamsville, New York, who helped pinpoint the exact location of the Sens's Neversink farm. Plus, I owe special thanks to Bob Hutton—Ed Sens's son-in-law, and his children, Kim Borghardt and Ken Hutton—Ed Sens's grandchildren. They helped substantiate my inquiries and added valuable personal insights that were not available anywhere else. If Bob had not shared the letters exchanged between Ed Sens and A. J. McClane, much of this information would be lost with time. I also wish to thank Eric Peper for additional insights on McClane and his *Field & Stream* column, "One for the Book." Without the valued help of all these folks these stories about Ed Sens in the following chapters would not have been possible.

Special thanks also to Beth Waterman of the Phoenicia Library and to Kathleen Myers, director of the Shandaken Historical Museum, for

---

[1] Roger Menard knew Ed Sens personally and met Sens through Harry Schadt, a mutual friend. In *My Side of the River: Reflections of a Catskill Fly Fisherman* (Hensonville, NY: Black Dome Press, 2002), he noted, "It was also on the Neversink that Ed Sens created some of his fly patterns that became well known to fishermen in the nineteen-thirties and forties. Years later, when I met Ed, I was fortunate enough to inspect some of his flies and discuss different tying methods with him" (p. 114).

their valued assistance on the Catskill Hollows chapter. I know others have assisted me also in various ways, though some unnamed in the body of the text. Your help and support was greatly appreciated. I also wish to thank those who allowed me to angle in their presence, without which some of these tales might not be told. But most importantly, I owe heartfelt appreciation to my wife, Lois, for putting up with me, allowing me to pursue this passion of mine. There is one chapter written with her in mind.

Additionally, I express my straightforward appreciation to authors cited in the footnotes utilized. Footnotes were included to acknowledge credit where credit was due, plus to allow readers the opportunity to dig deeper into specific topics, if so desired. Those works provided me enjoyable reading and often taken me on fond journeys. It is my genuine hope that these footnotes will do likewise for readers here. I also want to thank the Ashokan-Pepacton Watershed Chapter of Trout Unlimited for allowing me to reference a project report on their first Catskill Heritage Brook Trout study, which I participated in. Plus, sincere thanks to Bud Bynack, Joe Kosarek, and Roy Meyerhoff for reviewing the contents of what follows. Finally, some of the chapters within appeared in prior versions in the *Woodstock Times* or the *Gazette*, the newsletter of the Catskill Fly Tyers Guild. It is with earnest gratitude to those editors—Brian Hollander and Chuck Coronato, that with their permission these tales are retold here. Financial compensation was not received by me for any articles published elsewhere and recounted within. And special thanks to Bill Nicol—aka Stickball Finn, an original Jersey Boy— for allowing me use of his photo of the Antrim Lodge glass, from memories long since gone but not forgotten.

Contents

Tales from a Catskill Eddy and Other Trout Waters

The National Oceanic and Atmospheric Administration, NOAA, defines an eddy in the ocean as the circular motion of water, or a whirlpool, if you will. Trout-stream anglers come to know eddies as stream currents of circular movement that collect flotsam and jetsam that the water's revolving motion won't let go—things that collect with the passage of time and flow of life about it.

I've been caught in the eddies of life in the Catskills and the flows of the Catskill trout waters for over half a century now, along with the experiences of people and places and the histories and events that have accumulated there as I wandered environs many may only dream about, but where few ever journey. In *Ramblings of a Charmed Circle Flyfisher*, published in 2012, I explained to readers how I settled in these Catskill Mountains. What follows here are some of the things that have collected out of the flow of that life, based upon entries from years of angling logs and other misadventures, true stories, but sometimes told with poetic license, that unfolded during the last half century of earnestly fly fishing for trout, a task that was interrupted—but not stopped—by major open-heart surgery. If nothing else, I wanted to record happenings and various events that could be lost as we all return to the great current of time if left untold. In other words, these aren't just my stories, but they involve places, fly fishers, and the times the tales recount, collected from the flow of a Catskills' life.

Ed Ostapczuk

April 2nd, 2021

Daffodils

When I taught middle school math every year one of the teachers would sell daffodils in support of the American Cancer Society. As one of the first flowers that bloom each spring, daffodils symbolize rebirth and new beginnings. For those affected by cancer, just perhaps, daffodils represent hope for a future. They are among the first perennials to greet us each spring following winter's chill, brightening my wife's garden with their cheery yellow hues.

It was a late March afternoon with the month almost fully spent. While sitting outside on our back porch, I observed daffodils flowering in the garden and could sense nature transforming. Winter's snow was in retreat, with only grim gray patches to be seen in secluded corners of the yard. A gentle, soft spring rain dripped from tree limbs while pinging its way through downspouts attached to the house. Every now and again, a chipmunk scrambled through the rock wall, while comrade squirrels dug for acorns buried in a sleepy lawn.

A damp chill filled the late-day air as the terminus of March was upon us. Neighborhood dogs barked in the distance, annoyed by things unseen. Blades of grass struggled to awaken from winter's doldrums, to turn green once again, while mountain laurel readied to bloom and knobby woody arms from the kingdom of Plantae sprouted tiny green buds. Wood smoke circled about the chimneys of nearby houses, steely and wispy, intensely trying to climb through the dense spring air. Nature's silence was almost deafening as it sang choirs of rebirth and hope. Nature had been muted for months, but now begged to be heeded. Trout season would open next week, and I heard the daffodils speak to me. Soon, Little Black Stoneflies and Quill Gordons would follow.

Brightly, daffodils can inspire hope within us all, a rebirth with spring upon us and their association with a new trout season is no small wonder. As distinguished angling psychiatrist Paul Quinnett proclaimed in *Pavlov's Trout*, "Fishing is hope experienced. When it comes to the human spirit, hope is all. Without hope, there is no yearning, no desire for a better tomorrow, and no belief that the next cast will bring the strike. Without hope, there is no wonder, no mystery and no reason to bother travelling at all."[1]

So here's to all in search of hope and good fishing. May those days be many and your nets be full as daffodils bloom once again.

---

[1] Paul Quinnett, *Pavlov's Trout: The Incompleat Psychology of Fishing* (Sandpoint, ID: Keokee, 1994), p. 5.

A Bump, a Snag, and Deer Hunter's Camp

The first of every April is April Fools' Day, which is also the beginning of another New York state trout season. For years, I've wondered if there's any correlation in these two events. This date marks a rite of passage, no matter what local weather or stream conditions may be. Two such Opening Days come to mind. Both stories are retold below.

The first one is my story. While making ready for an Opening Day in 2015, I double checked the fishing gear stored in the back of my truck the previous night and was stunned to find the damp wading shoes frozen solid. Luckily, I discovered this minor inconvenience early and quickly relocated these icy shoes under the heater of the Tacoma's cab as I ventured forth. While passing the Chimney Hole parking area, it hit me. There were several vehicles already parked there; trout season was now in play. Contrary to popular opinion, there are truly only two seasons of every year: trout season and everything else. That's it—that's all she wrote. And my new season had finally arrived!

On through West Shokan, the local brooks were very low, with the mountain's snow still concealing much of the terrain. Plus, the county road was white from the salt that coated it. From Department of Environmental Conservation's Kanape Trailhead up past Peekamoose Lake, two seasons were clearly at odds with each other, winter and Opening Day. As I drove past Bear Hole Brook in the Peekamoose Valley Riparian Corridor, the tributary was missing, buried beneath massive ice and snow formations.

Along Rondout Reservoir, I paused long enough to sip coffee from my thermos while searching for bald eagles. I saw none, but observed numerous angler vehicles parked near the limited open water on New York City's reservoir. Now I was getting antsy. Once at Woodbourne, I noticed that two inches of fresh snow covered the landscape. It probably fell last night.

The Neversink was low, gin clear, and icy cold; newly formed skim ice lined the banks in many places. Though I sported high-tech thermal underwear and fleece wading pants, I really wished I had worn my wool trousers, which just had been dry-cleaned and put away until next winter. As I cast a small weighted streamer early on, ice clogged the guides of my cane fly rod. What a morning.

Nonetheless, I carefully fished several favorite pools with a small Black Leech streamer, slow and deep, deep and slow. In Rhododendron Pool, I felt a light bump, but repeated casts to the same spot produced nothing more. Moving along, soon enough, I drove the barb of the Leech into a solid take as my tip of the Battenkill doubled over. It was the most excitement I'd experience on the Neversink that day. But fortunately for me, I didn't damage the bamboo rod striking a submerged snag.

Trudging into to this isolated pool took some effort, because quite a bit of snow lay along the river banks. In many places, I managed to trek on top of the frozen stuff, but more times than not, I sank up to my knees. I'd relocate only once on the Neversink that day and was surprised by the number of anglers I encountered, well over a dozen, with even a couple fishermen above Hasbrouck, in what I call Deliverance

Country, where this part of the outing ended. I had high hopes there, but never even managed to nick a submerged stick again.

Afterward, while driving back toward home I saw a bald eagle sitting in its nest along the Rondout Reservoir. That's usually a good omen for me, and I still wanted to explore the Esopus Creek watershed somewhere, or else it wouldn't be much of an Opening Day. Eventually, I parked along a little mountain brook, a brook with no name except for the one a few locals know. It was low and clear, with midges about. At least there were some signs of life in the air.

The day was cold enough that there was minimal snowmelt in the creek. However, with ample snow along the banks, this was another physical workout negotiating the terrain in waders. Plus it was tough to discern if the rocks were just wet or ice coated.

They were ice coated, and I fell to the ground once after stepping on one. Tucked away in the woods, I finally reached the Deer Hunters' Camp Pool and was glad I did.

Fishing two weighted nymphs, a size 12 Epeorus on point with a size 14 Hare's Ear dropper, the first cast into the tiny pool produced a little brook trout that ate the Epeorus. I had several more hits and then decided to press on deeper into this snowy hollow with no signs of any tracks about. I dabbed two flies slowly upstream on a short, tight line in cold, skinny water. By the time this outing ended, five little wild brook trout came to hand in a snow-covered winter wonderland.

I enjoy environs like this more than one could imagine. The very origins of life can be found in depths of this Catskill hollow, with few signs of human intervention other than the deer hunters' camp, and those folks use it carefully, and only a couple of weeks each year.

That particular Opening Day, I wandered two different favorite watersheds, both buried in snow. But mine is not the only such tale of the beginning of a trout season. The one that follows is one of my favorites, disclosed to me by another Neversink trout fisher who has fished this tailwater since he was a teenager.

A young lad had his mother's permission to cut school one Opening Day, so he fished the Neversink with some buddies. The father of one of the friends worked for the highway department nearby and dropped them off to try their luck. Snow was still about, and the river was high and cold. However, they were determined to fish the beginning of a new trout season. As it turned out, these young men caught a few trout, even though they also had ice in their guides. But by midmorning, they were cold, so they decided to eat lunch while sunning on a large, mid-river rock.

As these four anglers munched sandwiches, shared soup, and told jokes, along came a man with a camera. From the bridge above them, he inquired if he could take their picture. Thinking nothing of this, they said, "Sure!"

It turned out that man was a *Times Herald Record* reporter, and their picture appeared in the newspaper the following day. Now back at school, individually, each boy was called into the principal's office and questioned about cutting classes the day before. Fortunately, one of the parents of these young Izaak Waltons informed the school's principal that they took the day off in the name of science to study trout.

The Opening Day of trout season comes but once a year. Snow or not, cold, muddy water or not, no matter your age, create your memories while you still can.

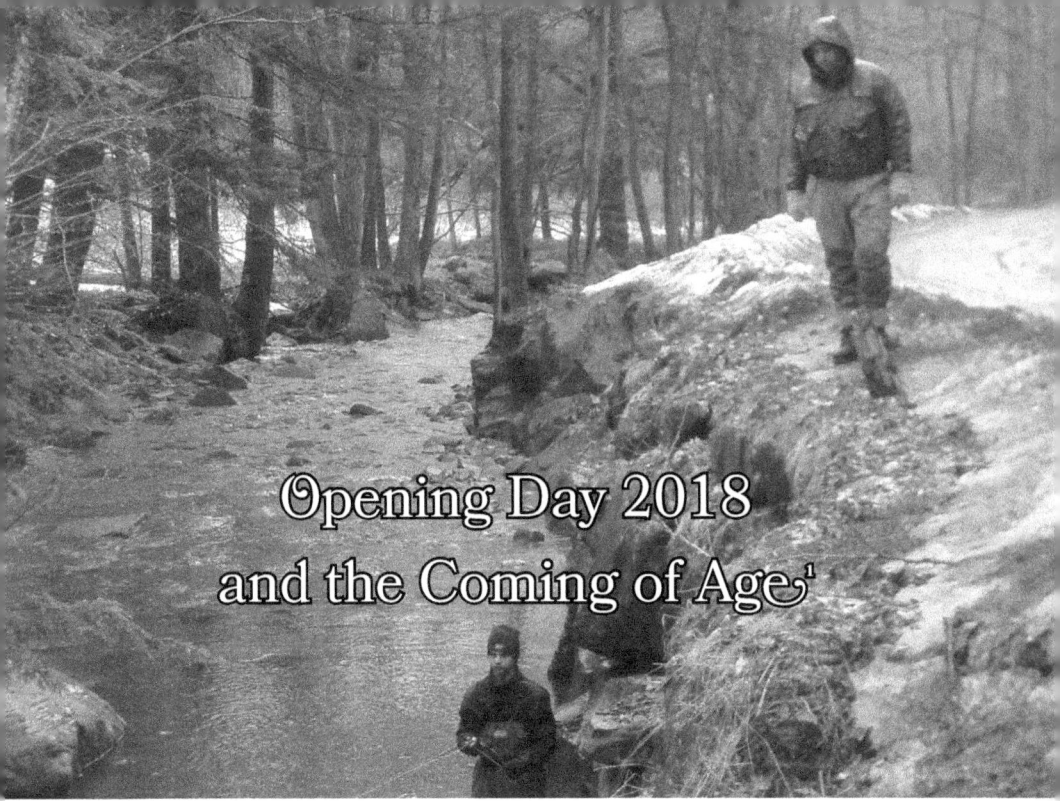

Opening Day 2018 and the Coming of Age[1]

W hat a winter we just experienced; a winter that wouldn't quit even now as our calendars inform us spring has officially arrived. If memory serves me correctly, December got nasty cold, as did January, with each month drier than normal. Both the National Oceanic and Atmospheric Administration and TV's Weather Channel reported that while winter temperatures over most of the globe were above average, the Northeast experienced near record cold weather.

It was so cold, we fired up our wood pellet stove before Thanksgiving, something we've never done before, while our garage heater turned on constantly. It was so cold, newspaper articles reported on frozen pipes and busy plumbers, who were booked solid. It was so cold, the ground froze, potholes blossomed in our roadways, while anchor ice formed in local streams. For anglers and wild trout, anchor ice is not good. It

---

[1] A version of this chapter appeared in the *Woodstock Times*, March 29, 2018.

can kill the aquatic insects that trout feed on; it can also impair last autumn's year class of freshly hatched brown and brook trout fry.

However, winter teased us; it played with our psyche with a total disregard for our mental well-being. February was one of the warmest Februarys ever. We even had a couple of seventy-degree days, followed by March madness: once again it got cold and snowed. More snow might have fallen in March than during the rest of winter. It was a winter that wouldn't go away, but anglers could take hope. Opening Day of another trout season was now upon us, the annual rite of passage and time finally to put winter behind us, no matter what the weather might bring. After all, not only is fishing "hope experienced," as Dr. Paul Quinnett said in *Pavlov's Trout*, but "catching a fish is hope affirmed."

I've enjoyed numerous Opening Days, including Opening Days for trout seasons in two or three different states the same year. Now a crusty ole angler, for me, Opening Day still brings time-honored traditions. For one, I have a special opening day hat—a hat purchased long ago in Rafalowsky's Men's Store, a hat similar to one sported by legendary Catskill angler Sparse Grey Hackle on the cover of his book *Fishless Days, Angling Nights*. And every Opening Day morning, before I leave for a day's adventure, my wife makes a hearty French toast breakfast and packs me a couple of fried-egg sandwiches to go along with my thermos of hot decaf coffee.

As I depart for the outing, I inform my bride where I'm heading, but she takes a strict oath not to divulge my whereabouts to anyone else. As my navy uncle used to say, "Loose lips sink ships," and who wants to be standing next to other anglers in icy-cold water, attempting to seduce their first trout of the new season. Thus, most years, I wander the Catskills solo on that first day; but some years are special, when I fish with a son and maybe a grandchild. On those occasions, catching a trout is secondary; it's much more satisfying to spend these special moments with family members.

Yes, I've participated in over fifty years of Opening Days, and they are all different. Most of the time, the event is not even close to being a good day to fish. Often ice has clogged the guides of my cane fly rod, or I have had to break through ice lining the creek's edge and crunch along a stream bank covered with snow. However, after the winter we'd had, I was really looking forward to the 2018 trout season. Still, I cannot help but think back to a New Jersey Opening Day in '69 and the Summer of Love. On that day, I came of age, a hard-core, dyed-in-the-wool fly fisher who forever swore off worm dunking and use of other bait. That Opening Day remains as fresh in my mind now as when it happened half a century ago.

On the 1969 opener, my now brother-in-law, Grover Koch, and I fished the Big Flat Brook River in northwestern New Jersey together. He fished bait, while for the first time ever, I took a different path and used a nymph, an unweighted Cooper Bug that I tied. From that day forward, I renounced worms and salmon eggs forever. The stream was overcrowded, as Jersey streams often are on Opening Days, but we were happy just to take part in that annual ritual.

I remember split shots plunking, bobbers bobbing, anglers hooting and howling, and hooked trout splashing and flopping on the bank and being caught all around me. I had all I could do just to get a decent drift through this piscatorial mess of slap-happy humanity. Eventually, things settled down because most other anglers limited out and left the water, while I caught and released but two small hatchery rainbows. I was content with my catch and proud that I had stayed the course, not succumbing to the urge of bait fishing.

As I surveyed my surroundings, there, resting on the bank, was Grover, watching me. At first, I felt a bit sorry for him, since he was no longer fishing, but I quickly asked him how he did, to which he responded, "OK. I caught and released twenty-three trout! How did you do?" At that moment, I knew my fly-fishing experiences could only improve. And simultaneously, a hard-core fly-fishing purist was born within me, something that I never regret.

Big Fish, Small Sizes and Saw Kill Wild Trout[1]

The headwaters of the Saw Kill Creek originate in a small lake, fed by feeder creeks and springs before flowing approximately twenty miles down through Greene and Ulster Counties, joining the lower Esopus Creek. Echo Lake, the river's source formerly known as Shue's Lake, sits in the Indian Head Wilderness Area between the shadows of Plattekill and Overlook Mountains. At one time bobcats, black bears, wolves, and whitetail deer were common cohorts in this setting. And it was reported that Native Americans used this lake as a base camp where brook trout once abound. Accounts written by both Alf Evers and Ed Van Put make mention of this jewel of a natural Catskill lake and stream. Yet when someone thinks of the Saw Kill these days, they probably don't think of it as a classic Catskill trout water. Plus, Father Time, urbanization, and Mother Nature have not been very kind to it.

During the many years I've wandered these Catskills I've learned

---

[1] A version of this chapter appeared in the *Woodstock Times*, March 31, 2016.

to fish its numerous trout streams, if by no other means than simply through the long, ongoing process of osmosis. Yet there was at least one stream that still haunted me. Over a period of four and a-half decades I'd fished the Saw Kill Creek at least a half dozen times and never once ever caught a single trout, much less nicked a fish.

I owe this obsession to Nick Lyons—yes, the noted author-publisher of fine angling books. I vividly recall Nick writing about his earliest angling days, fishing the East Branch of the Croton after taking a "five forty-five milk train" from Grand Central to Brewster. Well, I, too, eventually fished the East Branch Croton, following in his tracks and those of the late Art Broadie. And I caught a trout, though of hatchery derivation. I've always enjoyed reading about someone else's angling experiences and then trying to follow in their tracks. Nick Lyons also wrote about catching many trout in "his" Saw Kill Creek while poo-pooing my Esopus, writing it was never a favorite stream of his.

Heck, Nick is one of the best angling authors there is, and I've read most of the fishing accounts he ever wrote. So, I figured maybe there's something to this Saw Kill Creek. On the other hand, if you read Lyons's work, he's also the self-proclaimed master of piscatorial mishaps. So, if he can catch trout in Saw Kill Creek, then why can't I? And I'm not talking about a freshly planted hatchery trout. I want a wild fish.

For years, I ardently studied maps, asked questions of everyone who'd listen, and drove back roads along Saw Kill Creek from the golf course at the junction of Routes 212 and 375, in Woodstock, upstream. I even hiked into Echo Lake, the stream's source, hoping to resolve this issue, but sadly didn't accomplish that task. Then on the last day of June 2015 my good buddy, Tony Cocozza—aka Mr. Spundun, and I assaulted the Saw Kill Creek in Shady at the terminus of a dead-end dirt road lost in a hollow just a couple miles downstream of Echo Lake. While setting up, before descending into the hidden ravine below, the feeling was exhilarating, perhaps akin to the first time one kisses a member of the opposite sex. I was truly energized!

I'd never wandered this part of the stream at all, and the Saw Kill appeared to me to be up, running almost full bore and stained the color of gray sewer water. However, the setting was truly wild. It was every-thing I could have imagined in a mountain stream. The gully held a steep gradient of glacial drift and worn stream banks. Giant granite boulders craved out by the Ice Age were all about, cuddling gentle, undulating trout waters lined by a dark hemlock forest with tops that poked holes in the Catskill sky above. The setting appeared to be that of a Winslow Homer landscape as I fished a size 10 Martinez Black on point with a size 12 Prince Nymph dropper. When I got my first hit, I nearly wet the pants in my waders I wore. All these years, and finally I pricked a trout—a wild boy, no less— in Saw Kill Creek.

Sadly, we then fished the Saw Kill hard for some two hours that day, during which my flies nicked six fish, but I never touched one. It would take less than a week for me to return to the site of this endeavor because the thought of this recent failure was a constant stimulus pro-viding me reason enough to try again.

I was back once more by myself and that afternoon the stream was still slightly stained, but transported an easier, less dynamic flow. Once again, I fished a Martinez Black and Prince dropper—two weighted nymphs. And I could not have made a half dozen casts before I had a solid strike.

Almost instantaneously I lifted a wild brown through the air and quickly deposited it flopping on the wet, stony bank. Finally, years of groundwork were rewarded. On the very next cast, I caught a smaller fish, a wild brook trout. From that starting point upstream, I wandered perhaps some hundred and fifty yards of rich, foamy pocket water in forty-five minutes before a hemlock tree reached out and stole my Martinez Black. During the journey, I caught six browns and one brook trout, all but two on the Martinez Black, and not a trout over ten inches long, but all wild fish. These were still big, notable fish in the design of my priorities. At that point I quit. Mission accomplished!

This was the same Saw Kill that Nick Lyons wrote of in *Bright Rivers*. In the chapter titled "A Catskill Diary," he wrote:

14

The Sawkill is always a genial, clear, underfished creek, rather small and growing smaller each successive day of summer; some years the water simply vanishes — slipping between the rocks to some underground shelf and leaving small, unmoving, stagnant pools. At best, ten years ago, it provided a pleasant evening's spot-fishing for ten-inch browns, with always the chance of moving a holdover of some size on a delicate cast to some deeply undercut bank.[2]

Those were the words that fired the passion in my search of a Holy Grail, a Saw Kill wild trout all these many long years. Sadly, I don't think this brook is any longer quite what Nick Lyons wandered decades ago. Later that July day on the drive out of the hollow a certain emptiness set in. That said, I had never caught a wild trout in Chestnut Creek over Grahamsville way, either. Now that little brook popped up to the top of my bucket list.

---

[2] Nick Lyons, *Bright Rivers: Celebrations of Rivers and Fly-Fishing* (New York: J. B. Lippincott, 1977), pp. 78–79.

The Season of our Discontent

Climate change is here to stay unless we *Homo sapiens* wake up and address it. During the last few decades, the eastern Catskills have experienced an increase in the number of epic storms affecting the region, with 2011 bringing floodwaters of historic proportions. However, the tale below is about a flood and carnage that took place in early 2005.

The 2005 trout season began like so many before it. I was full of optimism and anticipation, with visions of dancing rainbows on the business end of my leader. Our regional streams were low and clear, with mountain peaks full of snowpack; only great expectations for that season filled my dreams. However, before the clock struck midnight to signal the arrival of Opening Day, rains came and stayed for days. Downpours washed away the snowpack, roads, railroad tracks, bridges, and even a few homes. And the precipitation opened an untold number of clay banks throughout the Esopus Creek watershed. The rains turned the Esopus brown, filling it with a red tide that lingered on through late summer. Plus, after April 1st each new moderate rainfall caused the Esopus Creek system to return to turbid storm conditions.

But the color of the water spoke only to the physical, visible issues caused by the spring flood; nothing alluded to how the storm almost broke the human spirit of mountain people intimate with the river. Business folk grew despondent, grown men cried, elected politicians cursed the rain, and anglers abandoned the Esopus in untold numbers. Thus began the long season of our discontent.

I avoided the Esopus like the plague that year. Who wants to wander turbid flows, anyway? The one time I fished the Esopus earlier season it was nothing like I remembered. The creek held a sad, somber look of devastation. I've always had the itch to fish it; however, it took nearly an entire trout season for that piscatorial rash to reappear. By August, conditions were finally settling down, except heavy rains pounded the region earlier that month, and many Esopus tributaries flowed off-color again. The stream at Five Arches Bridge once more took on the color of gray water flowing from a septic tank. Upstream of the hamlet of Phoenicia, the Esopus was much cooler, but brown and overflowing with recreational tubers. So I left my Subaru in the Chimney Hole parking lot, intent on fishing the waters I call Home, since I wasn't sure when the next angling opportunity might present itself.

The normally well-traveled path to the Chimney Hole was overgrown, lost in weeds. Muscle memory from over a hundred prior journeys blazed the unkempt trail for me. It was hot, close to ninety degrees, give or take a few. Nonetheless once at the Trestle I watched birds work the creek to a fever pitch, and to my pleasant surprise, stonefly shucks cluttered the rocks along the river's edge. Attaching a small streamer and large wet fly—a Fran Betters Mini Muddler Minnow and one of Ralph Hoffman's Black Bears —I slowly fished this water. Standing in the Esopus that early evening I lost all depth perception in water deeper than twelve inches. On my first pass through the riffle below the Trestle, I managed a small rainbow. On my second pass, I nicked only one fish, but it was great to be back home again.

Then I decided to wander down to the Chimney Hole. How can a season pass for a true Esopus Creek angler without at least one visit to this legendary fishing hole? On my way downstream, I was amazed to see how much of this section changed since the flood. Drifting my combination of submerged flies through the Chimney Hole, I soon felt the vicious strike of a really good fish, a fish measured in pounds, not inches. I set the hook at least twice and held my ground as this beast tore up the pool. It cleared water three times, showing the slender profile of a trout, slicing through the stream like a big rainbow, but we never got within fifty feet of each other to determine exactly what the fish was. Soon my line went slack and upon inspection I noticed the dropper fly was missing. Once again, a knot had failed me. Aroused I tossed a selection of streamers into the shaded, dull-gray water of the Chimney Hole for thirty minutes or more, but never felt the strike of another fish.

Eventually I found my way upstream to Big Bend, a favorite pool of the late Arnold Gingrich. Even though I had not seen a single rise, I fished a size 10 Ausable Wulff after observing stonefly shucks earlier. This dry fly managed to raise over a dozen fish. I landed a wild brown about ten inches, two small rainbows, including one with a big head and slender body, plus a beautiful, well-conditioned silver bullet—a 'bow that jumped about like its life depended on a strong fight. At 8:00 PM I quit, soaked to the bone from my own perspiration, but well satisfied.

Perhaps it was paradoxical that my 2005 Esopus Creek defining moment might have taken place in a legendary pool, on an early August evening, involving a fish I never landed, in a season that never got on track. Heaven knows how I missed my Esopus; I was one of those grown men who cried when the rains came. But that night, I stood in the red tide and made my choice; I would return to the Esopus at the next opportunity, red tide or not. That season was several months out of sync and the words of John Steinbeck's *The Winter of Our Discontent*, rang true that evening, "When a condition or a problem becomes too great, humans have the protection of not thinking about it. But it goes inward and minces up with a lot of other things already there and what comes out is discontent and uneasiness, guilt and a compulsion to get something—anything—before it is all gone." [1]

With climate change a reality, perhaps that outing in August of 2005 served as a gateway into days yet to come, unlocking a glimpse into the region's future. In those few short hours, I managed five small wild trout while losing perhaps my best Esopus Creek fish of the year, in a season of our discontent.

As of this writing, the table below lists the fourteen worst Esopus Creek floods ever recorded at the USGS Coldbrook gage, which has been in continuous operation since March 1932, a ninety-year period. During that time, there have been only eleven flood events that exceeded peak daily flows recorded on Christmas Day, 2020. And since the start of the twenty-first century on January 1st, 2001, five of these total twelve events—including Christmas 2020—or roughly 42 percent of the worst floods recorded at Coldbrook in the last ninety years, have occurred *in less than a quarter of that entire time period*. Clearly, large-storm events have become more frequent, significant, and intense, consistent with climate change predictions. With little doubt, these events have taken their toll on the Esopus Creek watershed and elsewhere in the Catskills.

---

[1] John Steinbeck, *The Winter of Our Discontent*, (New York: Viking Press, 1961), p. 155.

Esopus Creek, Coldbrook Gage
USGS 01362500
Historical Peak Daily Flow
(March 31, 1932 – December 25, 2020)

Date	Stream flow (cfs)	
2011-08-28	75,850	* Hurricane Irene
1980-03-21	65,300	
1951-03-30	59,600	
2005-04-03	55,200	
1933-08-24	55,000	
1955-10-15	54,000	* Hurricane Hazel
1966-01-19	53,600	
1987-04-04	51,700	
1957-12-21	46,900	
2010-10-01	43,550	
2010-12-01	39,830	
2020-12-25	39,100	
1936-03-12	38,500	
1984-04-05	37,400	

Autumn 2014

Come late autumn of many trout seasons, after leaves have fallen from trees and frost covers pumpkins, I'm often torn between fishing my Esopus as much as I can or trying something totally different, such as exploring New York City's Rondout Reservoir. New York City maintains six Catskill reservoirs as part of their two upstate water supply systems. The older Catskill system consists of only two reservoirs: the Schoharie and Ashokan—both important players in the Esopus Creek watershed. The newer Delaware system has four reservoirs: the Neversink, Pepacton, Cannonsville, and Rondout. The Rondout is the smallest of these and serves primarily as a collection basin for the other three impoundments before transporting water to thirsty downstate New Yorkers.

Consequently, the Rondout habitually receives cold-water diversions from tunnels connected to the other three supply basins, so the Rondout always has an ample supply of cold water, plus, these tunnels often deliver baitfish with their inflows. Hence, there are some large salmonids that make this water supply home, including browns, lakers, landlocked salmon, rainbows, and brook trout; though brown trout and lakers are the most prevalent fish of the group. And all of these fish can grow to large sizes. In September of 1992, the late Bill Kelly caught a fifteen-and-a-half-pound brown on a size 6 Rio Grande King wet fly, and it was Bill who first introduced me to fly fishing the Rondout Reservoir decades ago.

Typically, I wait for four conditions to be met before fishing this reservoir. First, I wait for autumn, specifically, the months of October or November, when brown trout are making ready to spawn. Second, rather than fish from a rowboat, I wade the shoreline of this impoundment, waiting until its volume drops to 90 percent of capacity or less. Third, I watch for tunnel diversions, that is, major inflows of water into this reservoir from the other Catskill reservoirs. During autumn when browns spawn, healthy water inflows often draw fish pursuing an upstream run, searching for gravel beds to reproduce. Plus, these inflows usually provide a source of food. And finally, this reservoir fishes best on cloudy, overcast, rainy days. I've never done well here when the sun is beating down on the water. Years may elapse when these conditions never collectively present themselves, in which case, I don't fish the Rondout Reservoir at all. However, when conditions are right, though they might last for only a couple weeks or even just a few days, the fishing can be the best of the season—in other words, outstanding. Then you had better make every effort to be present, since there are no guarantees when conditions might change again. The autumn of 2014 was one such time, and several accounts from my angling log are retold below.

October 16th. A substantial rain fell the night before, yet Rondout Reservoir still remained under 90 percent capacity. That day when I drove over Five Arches Bridge, the Esopus Creek was a muddy, high-flow mess. As I drove through Peekamoose along upper Rondout Creek, water flowed into it at many places, with numerous super-charged waterfalls, where I hadn't seen any flows for months prior. At New York City's reservoir, rain continued while I made ready, but when it came time to fish, sun poked out through the clouds. That could have been a game changer.

When fly fishing this impoundment, I always bring two special streamer boxes with flies tied just for here, many on size 2 Partridge Carrie Stevens 10X-long hooks. Over the years, a fish or two have totally demolished some of these large flies. A 9-foot 7-weight five-and-three-quarter-ounce Wright & McGill Granger Victory 9053 is my cane rod of choice. It's a real cannon and perfect for what it's asked to do.

On that particular day, the Rondout was totally devoid of human activity, but a handful of seagulls worked the Pepacton outflow, while a bald eagle circled overhead. The setting was uninterrupted and peaceful, yet one could get bored tossing big flies with a heavy rod and not much else happening. I typically catch only one trout for every three trips here. However, the late Bill Kelly told me the Rondout Reservoir is probably the best Catskill trout fishery there is and worth the effort. He should have known.

Wading this reservoir requires care and attention to detail, because the bottom hides many soft spots with air bubbles coming up, spots that could engulf you like quicksand. Initially, I fished a size 2 Winnipesaukee Smelt, throwing it out as far as I could toward the deep blue horizon. Zip! Then I replaced it with a Blue Clouser Minnow, working it slow and deep as I played the game of chuck and duck.

I was almost ready to quit when my rod doubled over, the fly line ripped from my hand. I was grateful for the 2X tippet. It would take a solid fifteen minutes to battle this brute, which took me into my backing once as I stumbled about the loose cobbles underfoot. Several times I altered the rod's angle, trying to pressure the fish and prevent it from running back into the main body of the reservoir. Battling a fish this big was unfamiliar territory for me—nothing like hauling in the six-inch brook trout I was used to catching. Eventually, I beached a large brown trout that posed as a football over twenty-two inches in length. This was my best trout of the season thus far, so upon its release, I was done fishing. Who could have wanted more?

October 18th. My wife and I planned to hike, but weather forecasters called for afternoon rain. So instead, we took a six-mile stroll along the Ashokan Reservoir before I fished the Rondout Reservoir again. Light rain fell as I packed my Tacoma, yet on the drive over several of New York State's trailhead parking lots were overflowing with hikers' vehicles despite the weather. Peekamoose Lake was on the rise, while small brook trout punched holes in its surface, feeding actively on this gloomy day.

Once at the Rondout Reservoir, I was disappointed, not finding any water diversions from the Delaware tunnels. Fishing would be a challenge. Initially, I tossed a Magog Smelt through a shallow channel that appeared to be flowing backward without the help of a tunnel diversion. Zip! Then I noticed fish working in the main body of the reservoir, far beyond my casting ability. I was annoyed that I wasn't prepared to fish from my rowboat, a boat I never use. My wife keeps reminding me of that fact.

Well, I watched and watched fish feed and it was a long enough drive from home, so determined I carefully picked my way out into the reservoir, as far as I could go, treading over the soft, mucky bottom. It was a slow go, with foul-smelling gaseous bubbles coming off the reservoir's soft floor. At times, I had to backtrack or risk a leg being swallowed up by the bottom, cementing me in place.

Once settled in, I chucked a small, size 8 black Conehead Woolly Bugger as far as I could. Soon I watched a wake follow my retrieve, but I only nicked that fish. Then to my disappointment, I caught a small yellow perch. Yet I stayed the course and soon watched a "Moby Dick" porpoise in the water several feet beyond where I could reach.

Ever so carefully I waded out even farther, over the mucky bottom, even deeper yet. A few more casts and there was an explosion on my Woolly Bugger, but I missed the strike. But with several fish still active, it wasn't too long before I hooked and caught a fat, round brown trout that barely fit in my landing net. Negotiating my way slowly back to shore, I measured this fish three times. It was twenty-inches long on the button and real porky.

After releasing the fish, I waded back out into the deep water as far as I could go. But sadly the sun came out, wind kicked in, and feeding trout disappeared. So I quit. Another Rondout outing was in the books.

October 22nd. I never saw a vehicle on the road from West Shokan to Sundown that morning. A definite chill sat over Peekamoose, while the mountain forest was only woody sticks pointing toward the sky. Raindrops coated my truck's windshield, while wood smoke permeated the mountain air on this dull, late-season October day. A change of seasons was definitely upon us.

New York City's Rondout Reservoir sat under a cloud-choked sky as I scouted the various tunnels for water diversions from other Catskill reservoirs. I only found one flow, perhaps a tad too heavy to fish effectively, but still, it was a good sign and my lone option.

The reservoir was up since my last visit on Sunday. Places I could carefully wade then were now far underwater, turning mushy and soft, very soft, and over my waders. I tried, but the reservoir's bottom was intent on swallowing me up, so I didn't persist down that avenue. Confined to a small sandbar, I fished alternating with three reservoir favorites: a Magog Smelt, Jack Gartside's Floating Minnow pattern, and a Winnipesaukee Smelt. Zip!

Well, not exactly. Using the 9053 Wright & McGill Granger, I tossed the Winnipesaukee Smelt as far as I could into the main body of the reservoir. On one cast, a broad, silver-sided fish swirled behind it, punching a hole into the water's surface the diameter of an old-fashioned hula hoop. Sadly, I never touched that fish. But it got my heart pumping and adrenaline flowing.

I watched a bald eagle circle overhead. That's always a good piscatorial omen for me, and so, it was today. The Rondout is often "the place of a hundred casts" or more, but it can be well worth it, and that was the reason I was there that day.

Finally, I attached a Blue Clouser Minnow, by far my favorite Rondout fly. I fished it slow and deep, doing nothing at all until I tossed it into the heart of a fast-water slot. The reservoir exploded as my streamer tried to swing through it, and I was fast into a good fish that put a deep bow into my old cane rod while taking yards of line besides.

Fortunately, my tippet was 2X, 6-pound-test material, because at one critical point, I leaned hard into the fish as it tried sliding beneath an underwater snag. Using as much pressure as possible, eventually I turned the battle in my favor. Soon I could see that I would not be able to net or beach that brown. Instead, I grabbed the trout in front of its tail like a salmon, dragging it up on the sandy bank. It measured twenty-six inches in length.

That brown was the best Catskill fly-rod trout I ever caught, three inches longer than any other. With that, I quit. On that soggy, late-autumn day, I got lucky. The swirl alone early on would have satisfied me, but that fish was special. The reservoir was coming up and paradise would be lost in the wet days ahead, as the Rondout began exceed the 90 percent capacity threshold I fancy. Up to that point, it was my best season ever fly-fishing this reservoir. I had caught at least one twenty-inch or larger brown trout on each visit and now my best Catskill trout ever. Ole Catskill Bill Kelly had been smiling down on me and I will never, ever forget that it was Bill Kelly who introduced me to fly fishing this body of water.

October 25th. By now word must have gotten out about the Rondout Reservoir, because several anglers were fishing in "my spot." The reservoir was definitely rising, because New York City was diverting volumes of water into the Rondout from their other Delaware supply sources. The day was sunny, but heavy winds were forecast for the next day. Thus, I would make do finding a place to toss my flies on what would be my last visit of this season.

The place I chose to fish held a good flow coming into the reservoir, with no one else about. Initially I used a Blue Clouser Minnow, but in my haste tied a poor knot attaching it to the leader. It didn't take long, maybe a half dozen casts, when a football-fat brown, easily twenty inches long and probably longer, was almost at my feet. Then the knot failed, leaving the Clouser in that trout and me with a curlicue on the end of the tippet.

So, I attached another Blue Clouser Minnow and soon there was another brown, about sixteen inches long at my feet before that fly pulled out. At least this time the knot held. I kept chucking the Clouser and nicked several more fish, landing five relatively small browns eleven to thirteen inches long, mere babies for this body of water.

Later sun gave way to cloudy conditions and I replaced my overworked Clouser Minnow with a Winnipesaukee Smelt, which I worked high in the water column. That fly accounted for four more brown trout, from a foot long to fifteen inches in length. Then I fished a Magog Smelt missing a fish using it, but that was it. By late afternoon, fishing really slowed down.

However, for one final time I reattached the Clouser, tossing it out as far as possible. That resulted in a solid hookup with a heavy fish. It fought hard for quite a while, but it just didn't feel quite like a trout. Eventually, I beached a nineteen-inch largemouth bass. Upon its release, I was done fishing the Rondout for the day and year. On the day, I had caught nine small brown trout and one nice largemouth bass. And I have to admit that bass fought like a champion, putting the efforts of the brown trout I caught to shame.

During the days that followed, the reservoir's volume increased too much, and it was no longer practical to wade from shore. When the Rondout Reservoir fishes right, it's magical. There's nothing like it in these Catskill Mountains.

Believe it or Not

"Believe it or not" is a phrase that implies the unbelievable unfolding before one's very eyes. And, like many avid fly fishers, I have had my share of such moments. The year was 2015, and it was mid-June day, when on the prior day rain fell in bucket proportions. During that deluge, Slide Mountain stood tall preventing the monsoon from leaving and causing both branches of the upper Neversink and the Claryville main stem to increase their flows by sixfold, per the local USGS stream gage. At Coldbrook the Esopus Creek tripled its flow, which ran brown, as brown can be. This didn't really matter much to me because, as I used to tell my buddy Rich, I can always find a place to trout fish in these mountains. And with more rain and thunderstorms in the next day's weather forecast, I knew I had better take advantage of what I can, when I can. Thus, I decided to explore the Neversink downstream of New York City's Catskill reservoir. On the trip over, the many waterfalls along the upper Rondout Creek were supercharged; water, water all about, producing quick, heavy downstream flows as a foggy mist sat atop the icy cold and slightly stained Rondout.

In a total contradiction of reality, upon arriving at my destination I found the Neversink low, very much unlike other Catskill rivers, but slightly stained under a cloud-choked sky. A few sporadic risers were on top picking off Light Cahills that drifted by. Yet for better or worse I had already decided to toss my small Black Leech in pursuit of big brown trout. I have too many fond memories of vicious strikes under similar conditions burned into the fabric of my mind not to fish a Black Leech.

Soon I experienced two strong pulls on the little streamer, but missed them both. Then I nicked and rolled a few other trout before hooking a good brown of some seventeen inches in length. Sadly, we also parted company, so I changed flies just in case the barb on the Leech was dull or defective. By the time I accomplished that minor task, I had nicked six good fish, but touched none.

Next I decided to wandered upriver to a different pool and venue. There I managed another strong strike that parted the light tippet securing my fly. So, I attached a stouter tippet and yet another Black Leech, now slowly working my way downstream. What happened next is the "believe it or not" moment. My background is that of an engineer who eventually taught middle school math, so I'm not articulate enough to make this stuff up. Plus, I have a photograph to support this fishy tale.

As I waded the tailwater, casting, fishing, looking at my fly, wading and casting, moving slowly along, I tumbled into the Neversink on all fours. There I was, on my hands and knees like a dog in less than two feet of moving water, but trying to stay still and stand up. It wasn't deep at all, but my 8-foot Battenkill was on the bottom of the river, underneath me. I wasn't worried about myself, but deeply concerned over the state of the bamboo fly rod. Slowly and carefully, I stood up, trying mightily not to damage the Battenkill or take any more water into my soggy waders. The fly rod was fine, but as I lifted it, putting tension on the line, I felt resistance and thought my Leech had snagged bottom. However, to my great surprise, the Black Leech had firmly planted itself in the jaw of a twenty-one-and-a-half-inch rainbow trout!

Stunned and dripping wet, I played that trout as best I could, eventually slipping it into my net, though the net could not hold the entire fish. As I stumbled back to shore, I nearly fell in again. Clearly, this was not one of my most graceful moments on a trout stream. Maybe the rainbow struck due to a "Leisenring lift" caused by my standing upright, or more likely it was just dumb luck. But I'll say this much for dumb luck, it's far better than no luck or bad luck, for sure.

Yogi and the Fat Lady[1]

The summer of 2016 was warm, very dry, and a season to remember for all the wrong reasons. Three of the Esopus Creek's four scheduled recreational water releases were cancelled due to the lack of rain and water. During August the Shandaken Tunnel discharged flows with water temperatures in the mid-seventies, while the USGS Coldbrook gaging station reported daily river temperatures spiking into the eighties. Fortunately, Catskill streams have the advantage of diurnal fluctuating water temperatures due to the dampening effect of cool mountain evenings, so our wild trout often find some relief from these torrid conditions at night.

However, late that summer New York City's Schoharie Reservoir volume dropped below seven percent capacity, with inflow to that water-supply impoundment approaching an all-time low. Not only was the amount of water being diverted through the Shandaken Tunnel in jeopardy, but those skinny, warm diversions became extremely turbid.

---

[1] A version of this chapter appeared in the *Woodstock Times*, December 8, 2016.

The Shandaken Tunnel inflows were shearing silt from the bottom of an almost dry Schoharie Reservoir, while Esopus Creek tributary inflows were virtually nonexistent. Local Catskill watershed conditions were very, very sad indeed.

By late November, much-needed rain finally found its way into the Catskills, with creeks and rivers on the rise once more, dragging fresh snowmelt downstream with it. Below the Shandaken Tunnel the Esopus Creek held a tannish tint, yet upstream of Big Indian, it was relatively clear, carrying only an aqua snowmelt hue. Recent snowfall had all but disappeared from the high peaks, given warm weather and steady rain.

What bothered me most was on November 30th trout season would close at midnight, making a tough ending to a very tough year. Unlike Opening Day, on these final days there were no more tomorrows, no more redoes or reruns, no more second chances. It was then or never— or wait until next year. As the late, great Yankee Yogi Berra once said, "It ain't over till it's over," but it would be over at midnight on November 30th, 2016. The fat lady had begun singing, and her voice resoundingly echoed throughout the wooded Esopus Creek headwaters and mountain valleys.

On that last November day, I briefly gave thought to fishing New York City's Rondout Reservoir, but my heart really belonged to Esopus Creek during trout season's final hurrah. Early morning rain fell again as I drove NY 28 northwest, up into the mountains. Upriver of the Portal, the Esopus was flowing full again, but angry, stained, and cold. The creek was on a constant rise in the Big Indian–Oliverea Valley. On that final day, the upper Esopus supported a healthier flow than when I had fished the much larger Beaverkill River just earlier that month. Thus, I invested much of my time just searching for fishable water.

To get down into the trout's zone, I fished a short, tight line, dead-drifting a black size 8 Conehead Woolly Bugger on point with a size 12 weighted Prince Nymph dropper. Probing three favorite end-of-season locations, this combo produced the same results, nothing! Yet

I knew my flies had to be drifting over wild fish, because had I caught trout there as recently as Saturday just past.

High water, cold water, stained water I can handle, but experience has taught me the hard lessons of fishing snowmelt. I firmly believe the shock of cold water, coupled with a drop in pH from melting snow adversely affects trout, putting them off their feed.

That outing finally ended in the small water that I love to wander. Initially, nothing was doing in the best-choice locations. My mindset started just going through the piscatorial motions, not really expecting to catch anything at all, but then I caught a tiny wild brook trout, soon followed by another. Eureka! Working my way upstream, I eventually reached the Brook Trout Hole. Not much was doing there, except for a fish I spooked in the tailout, plus volumes of woody debris that spun about in the foamy froth of the isolated, miniscule pool's head. Then I caught my last Esopus Creek trout of 2016, one more brookie before quitting at noon for the day, and the season.

On that final day, I worked my Esopus hard for several hours, managing to detect but a few feeble hits, catching only three small wild brook trout. On Opening Day, many months prior I also managed to catch several small wild brook trout in a different Esopus Creek tributary. Hence, I had come full circle during this season.

Rain fell steadily and a ghostly fog ate the mountain peaks as I hiked up the steep incline along an old stone wall from the belly of the forest ravine below. It was a good day and I probably had experienced the best the Esopus had to offer because the stream was on the rise again. I was done fishing the Esopus for the season. And while there were enough exceptions, loopholes, and technicalities in angling regulations, I wasn't fully done fishing for the year—not quite yet. But the number of angling outings that laid ahead at that juncture didn't require all the fingers on one hand to count.

So 2016 was a complicated season for the Esopus Creek trout fishery. It started in grand fashion with a goodly number of wild rainbows caught from mid-April through late June. Then the creek warmed and became turbid all summer. Once it cooled and cleared again with the Portal closed, the prolonged dry spell caused the New York State Department of Environmental Conservation to close angling below the Shandaken Tunnel in early November. Yet trout were still to be had upstream of the Portal. With regard to the Esopus, trout season, and that last outing, it's been written, "So perhaps many of us are creatures of habit, followers of rituals. The opening and last day of each trout season are just part of the fabric of our lives. And I guess it's all the other outings between these bookend rituals that can become commonplace, lost in the fragments and dark places of our angling minds if allowed to happen; but these two days are clearly special."[2]

That day's outing was special and so is the Esopus Creek. On that last day, the fat lady did sing and Yogi nailed it.

---

[2] Ed Ostapczuk, *Ramblings of a Charmed Circle Flyfisher* (Bloomington, IN: Xlibris, 2012), p. 178.

ED. SENS
Custom Flies

Ed Sens, the Forgotten
Catskill Fly Fisher[1]

Who was Ed Sens?

Numerous celebrated angling authors credited Ed Sens for having influenced their thinking and for making significant fly-fishing contributions, nymph patterns in particular.

Ernest Schwiebert, in *Nymphs, Volume I*, provides the most complete single source of information available about this often-forgotten fly fisher. Sens's father, also named Edmund Sens, but referred to as "Pop Sens," purchased a large farm along the upper Neversink in the vicinity of Claryville. There, young Sens befriended Herm Christian, Edward Hewitt, and other notable Neversink fly fishers. According to Schwiebert, Ed Sens became quite a proficient night angler, catching many large brown trout on his Giant Stone Fly.

In *The Masters on the Nymph*, Schwiebert wrote, Sens was a "solitary genius who fished the Catskills, and his work resulted in a superb series of nymphs keyed to our better-known mayfly patterns.

---

[1] Versions of this chapter, and three following chapters, first appeared in the *Gazette*, newsletter of the Catskill Fly Tyers Guild beginning in June 2013.

His nymphs trace their lineage almost directly to Skues and are perhaps the most popular series available."[2] Sens never published these patterns or any of the results of the extensive research he did on the entomology of trout-stream insects, but Ray Ovington did so in his *How to Take Trout on Wets and Nymphs* and other works. Schwiebert added, "Sens, however, also added two completely original imitations of hatching caddis flies and started a revolution that still continues in the work of fishermen like Leonard Wright and Larry Solomon."[3] Schwiebert also noted that he, too, owed "a debt to the pioneer work."[4] Thus, as Schwiebert declared, "innovations introduced by Sens did not stop with the popular mayfly hatches, ... he must also be celebrated for his revolutionary imitations of emerging sedge pupae. . . . Sens was clearly ahead of his time."[5] Indeed in *Matching the Hatch* Schwiebert gave credit to Ed Sens for two caddis pupa patterns and a stonefly pattern he included in that book. But perhaps the highest compliment Ernest Schwiebert paid this fly fisher was, "The knowledgeable reader is left to wonder what a wonderfully original manuscript might have been written had Sens understood the potential of his theories and fieldwork, and had elected to prepare the book himself," rather than Ovington.[6]

But Ovington initially gave Ed Sens his due. In *How to Take Trout on Wet Flies and Nymphs*, Ovington, a noted angling author and outdoor writer for the *New York World Telegram and Sun*, called Ed Sens "one of the most successful nymph fishermen in the United States."[7] In his *Young Sportsman's Guide to Fly Tying*, Ovington wrote: "Many anglers have come up with killing patterns such as those in the preceding chapter. To these, invented by Eddy Sens, I can give my

---

[2] Ernest G. Schwiebert, "The Evolution of the Nymph," in *The Masters of the Nymph*, ed. J. Michael Migel and Leonard M. Wright, Jr. (Garden City, NY: Nick Lyons Books, 1979), p. 31.

[3] Ibid.

[4] Ibid.

[5] Ernest G. Schwiebert, *Nymphs, Volume I: The Mayflies* (Guilford, CT: Lyons Press, 2007), p. 86.

[6] Ibid., p. 87.

[7] Ray Ovington, *How to Take Trout on Wets and Nymphs* (Rockville Center, NY: Freshet Press, 1974), p. 81.

wholehearted approval. They have taken fish for me when all else has failed. My friends who have experimented with them are convinced of their killing qualities."[8] In *The Trout and the Fly*, Ovington also called Sens "my mentor, responsible for many of the patterns featured in my various books, a meticulous German who tied to match his personality."[9] He goes on to credit Sens (and eventually himself) with extending the "great work" of Preston Jennings and Art Flick. Both the 1951 and 1974 revised version of *How to Take Trout on Wets Flies and Nymphs* provide detailed nymph patterns developed by Sens for all the great Catskill hatches. However, in 1969, when Ovington published *Tactics on Trout*, he modified some of the Sens's patterns into "Ovington versions," although he still referred to Ed Sens as a "fly-tyer extraordinaire."[10] Though Sens and Ovington once held a fondness for each other, these changes reflected a rift that developed between the two men.[11]

Schwiebert and Ovington were not the only angling authors to sing high praises of Ed Sens. In *The Challenge of the Trout*, Gary LaFontaine declared, "The initial attempt at specific imitation of the caddis pupalform was an innovation of Edward Sens less than twenty-five years ago. These simulations of two Eastern species, *Rhyacophila lobifera* and *Psilotreta frontalis*, were listed by Ray Ovington."[12] And in *Caddisflies*, LaFontaine noted that Sens was a fly tyer for Jim Deren's Angler's Roost in New York City and had created "one of the best known of these early pupa imitations" calling Sens "a serious student of entomology."[13] Though LaFontaine was wrong about Sens's first

---

[8] Ray Ovington, *The Young Sportsman's Guide to Fly Tying* (New York: Thomas Nelson & Sons, 1962), p. 92.0

[9] Ray Ovington, *The Trout and the Fly* (New York: Hawthorn Books, 1977), p. 25.

[10] Ray Ovington, *Tactics on Trout* (New York: Alfred A. Knoff, 1969), p. 315.

[11] Robert Hutton, personal communication, November 23, 2016. According to Schwiebert, the Sens-Ovington connection was a chance meeting at the 1946 sportsman's exposition. Ernest St. Clair, who collected nymphs with Sens and also tied for Jim Deren, persuaded Sens to set up aquariums with nymph specimens, and that caught the attention of Ovington, an outdoor writer. See Schwiebert, *Nymphs, Volume I*, p. 87.

[12] Gary LaFontaine, *Challenge of the Trout* (Missoula, MT: Mountain Press, 1976), p. 110.

[13] Gary LaFontaine, *Caddisflies* (New York: Nick Lyons Books, 1981), p. 102.

name, the translucent appearance of his own Sparkle Pupa patterns can be traced back to Sens's nymphs. Leonard Wright, Jr., shared a recognition of Sens's influence in *Fishing the Dry Fly as a Living Insect* when he remarked that "the Ed Sens pupal imitations represent one of the few American attempts to deal seriously with caddis flies in any form."[14] Gary Borger also recognizes the work of Ed Sens in *A Guide to Food Organisms of the Trout* and *Designing Trout Flies*, as does Rick Hafele in *Nymph-Fishing Rivers and Streams*.[15]

So how can a legendary Catskill fly fisher and tyer who once drew high praise from numerous pillars of this pastime end up forgotten by most modern-day fly fishers? And, how can these same angling authors not even know Sens's correct name? Only Schwiebert, in his 2007 edition of *Nymphs*, referred to Ed Sens by his full accurate proper name: Edmund William Sens. I'll answer these questions in subsequent chapters.

---

[14] Leonard M. Wright, Jr., *Fishing the Dry Fly as a Living Insect* (New York: E.P. Dutton, 1972), p. 21.
[15] Rick Hafele, *Nymph-Fishing Rivers and Streams: A Biologist's View of Taking Trout below the Surface* (Mechanicsburg, PA: Stackpole Books, 2006), p. 4.

Ed Sens, the Man[1]

Some say the Catskill Rivers are the birthplace of American flyfishing, If so, then the Neversink is a cradle. Starting with waters emanating from Slide Mountain, the tallest peak, a long list of distinguished trout fishers called this river home and once cast their flies upon it. The portfolio of dignities includes Theodore Gordon, Edward R. Hewitt, Herm Christian, Larry Koller, and Leonard M. Wright, Jr.. Plus, anglers such as George M. L. La Branche, Ray Bergman, John Atherton, R. Palmer Baker, Arnold Gingrich, Sparse Grey Hackle, Ernest Schwiebert, and William H.—Catskill Bill—Kelly should not be ignored, either. And then there was Edmund William Sens, the forgotten Catskill fly tyer. Let's get acquainted with Ed Sens the man.

Edmund William Sens was born on June 24, 1914, and died on June 6th, 2003. He lived his entire life in the Bronx, where he married Helen Mary Elliffe (1916–1997) on January 20th, 1937. Sens worked as a

---

[1] Quoted family references, and that of Roger Menard, in this chapter were obtained from various personal correspondence received and kept.

maître d' at the Oyster Bay Restaurant in New York City, owned by his father. When his father became ill at the onset of the Great Depression, that resulted in young Edmund dropping out of college and the eventual financial failure of the restaurant in July of 1940. Sens was also an Abercrombie & Fitch employee, a fly tyer at Jim Deren's Angler's Roost, and a Catskill guide. He was an innovative tyer, skilled amateur entomologist, cane rod maker, and an outstanding angler for both trout and striped bass. He sometimes demonstrated fly tying at the Sportsman Show in the Grand Central Palace in New York City, where he might be seen tying flies with Elizabeth Greig (1902–1996), one of America's most accomplished female tyers.

He was probably one of the first important nymph fishers ever to wet a line in the legendary rivers of the Catskills. The fact that he never wrote a book leaves us to view him only through the eyes of others, and as the previous chapter documented, he was recognized as a serious Catskill fly fisher in the 1930s and 1940s, during the time when his father owned a farm on the Neversink near Claryville where Sens fished and grew to know other noted Catskill anglers. But then things changed, and Ed Sens gave up trout fishing, soon to become a very proficient striped bass angler. Was it World War II gas rationing, the economy, a budding new angling interest, or other personal factors that led Sens to this shift in angling? Or perhaps all of these factors brought about change, depriving Catskill trout fishers of a highly talented resource.

The two-hundred-plus acre farm along the banks of the Neversink was situated upriver of Hewitt's Big Bend Club, downstream of the white Claryville Reformed Church, where Theodore Gordon's funeral service took place, and just downstream of the New Your State Department of Environmental Conservation Public Fishing Rights section at the former 4-H Camp Pine property. I was able to pinpoint the location with the help of Sens's family members, plus the Time and the Valleys Museum tax maps. Pop Sens sold the farm in the late 1940s due to advancing years and poor health. After the farm's sale, Ed had no place to stay when fishing the Catskills, because the roads were not the best then, and travel to the Catskills was not easy. As of early 2017, there was a sign in front of the old farmhouse that read, "Halls Mills House 1913," and as of that date, the property was owned by the Schoenburg family and leased to Neversink Farm, an organic vegetable farm.

So Ed Sens's Neversink connection is quite clear and very strong. Schwiebert wrote that "there were traces of trophy brown trout bodies on the boards in the old barn on the Sens property."[2] Many of these trout were taken while night fishing with his Giant Stone Fly, a fly pattern that first caught my attention in the 1960s while reading *Matching the Hatch*. Even the *New York Times* wrote about large Neversink brown trout that Sens caught night fishing with this fly. Sens's Giant Stone Fly might have been his favorite pattern, according to his son-in-law Bob Hutton. And no one can erase from angling literature what has already been written regarding Sens's trout-fishing genius.

About the time his parents sold the family Neversink farm, while he was working at Abercrombie & Fitch as a tackle salesman and special-order fly tyer, Ed met a "surf fishing fanatic" named Mike "Stretch" Olenick, who invited Sens to surf fish with him, and the thrill of catching twenty-to-thirty-pound fish, coupled with the long, hassle-ridden drive to the Catskills, apparently influenced his piscatorial thinking. Sens would become a very knowledgeable and highly revered striped bass saltwater angler, and he gave up trout fishing on a regular basis in the early 1950s, though he would occasionally do some in the years to come and always enjoyed talking about it, according to his family members.

Sens became an affiliate of the Long Island Surf Fishing Club, where he won many angling contests and met Al Reinfelder, a highly respected Long Island striped bass angler. Reinfelder gave credit to Sens for his own personal angling development. In a Reinfelder memorial that appeared in the September 1973 issue of *Field & Stream* (p. 124), George Reiger wrote, "Under the tutelage of Ed Sens, a fabled Catskills stream guide who switched his allegiance to saltwater and

---

[2] Ernest G. Schwiebert, *Nymphs, Volume I: The Mayflies* (Guilford, CT: Lyons Press, 2007), p. 84.

striped bass just before World War II, Al became the leading bridge and shore fisherman of his generation."

Reinfelder was a noted saltwater angler-conservationist, a founding member of the Striped Bass Fund, Inc., and the author of fishing articles for *Long Island Fisherman Magazine* and the book *Bait Tail Fishing*. Reinfelder drew high praise from Robert H. Boyle in Dick Russell's book *Striper Wars* and is the subject of Chapter 20, "The Commando," in George Reiger's *Profiles in Saltwater Angling*—clearly a list of credentials as impressive as those of Ed Sens himself when it comes to striped bass.

The fact that both Ray Ovington and Al Reinfelder awarded Sens credit for their personal development as anglers in their own fresh and salt water environments speaks volumes for Sens's own angling abilities. Sens's ability to convey instruction to others was celebrated; his friends among the striped bass anglers referred to him as "Pappy Sens." As of this writing, various magazine articles, books, and online saltwater forums still mention Ed Sens and his influence on saltwater angling.

I had opportunity to gather firsthand materials about Ed Sens from several folks who knew him personally. Ed Sens's granddaughter, Kim Borghardt, offered valued information and introduced me to other family members. Kim wrote that when she was born, "Ed had pretty much given up fly fishing, though he had a 'back room' in the apartment where he kept his fly-tying equipment, and would occasionally show me how." She went on to say that he was "very meticulous about his flies," and she admired "the dedication and patience he took in everything he did." Kim added that she had "plenty of opportunity to go fishing with him at all hours of the day and night, despite Grandma's insistence that it wasn't right for girls to come home stinking of fish." Not surprising was this comment: "Growing up, he instilled in his children and grandchildren a love of fishing." But perhaps her most powerful and impressive comment about Sens was, "He was a great man, someone who understood that the joy of living was more important than making money." She also noted that her grandfather was very involved working for legislation to protect the striped bass he came to love. Clearly, Sens was an individual who embraced life to its fullest.

Ken Hutton, Kim's brother and Ed Sens's grandson, wrote that "Grandad was an exceptional man and full of wisdom. A serious angler indeed who thought through every step and investigated his craft with passion." He added, "I remember Grandad taking me out on the Neversink as a kid and wading chest deep in the cold, running waters. He said it was the only way to reach the trout and instructed me how to cast up against the flow of the river and allow the fly to sweep downstream and be taken in the swift eddy currents." Ken also confirmed that Sens "did indeed stop fly fishing to concentrate on saltwater striped bass fishing," adding that Sens was the steadfast teacher.

Bob Hutton, Ed Sens's son-in-law, also was a vital source of information about Sens. Hutton trout fished and chased stripers with Sens, becoming an accomplished saltwater angler himself. Bob said Sens was "the first fly fisherman I ever fished with." He singled out Sens's "attention to fine detail." He was a "perfectionist" and excellent angler, both in fresh and saltwater. Hutton fondly added, "He was my fishing buddy, father figure, and mentor." Hutton confirmed that after Pop Sens sold the Neversink farm, it "became a hassle" for Sens to fish in the Catskills, but that Ed would continue to talk trout fishing at the drop of a hat; it was inbred in him. Both Sens and Hutton would occasionally fish the Neversink after the farm's sale. Bob disclosed it was often suggested that Sens write a book on his nymph patterns and research, but Sens did not want to invest the necessary time to complete such an undertaking. Hutton also revealed that Sens fished the Miramichi for Atlantic salmon and was quite the bamboo rod builder, plus owner of several Leonards and a Hiram Hawes cane rod that he kept long after he stopped fly fishing for trout.

Roger Menard, a Catskill Fly Tyers Guild member and author of *My Side of the River* also offered the following, "We had good conversation on several occasions about fly tying and Catskill fishing, particularly the stretch of water that Ed's father owned on the Neversink." Roger added, "Because Ed was such a skilled fly tyer in imitating natural insects and because of his ability to choose just the right fly-tying materials in so doing makes him an important contributor to the 'Golden Age' of the Catskills. I believe that his contributions should be recognized and preserved with the Catskill angling history and his name should be included in the long list of Catskill fly tyers."

The Practical FLY Fisherman

The McClane Letter[1]

A. J. McClane was a freshwater and saltwater angler extraordinaire, author of numerous books, skilled fly tyer, artist, gourmet chef, explorer, and the celebrated *Field & Stream* fishing editor. Possibly his best angling works were *The Practical Fly Fisherman* and *McClane's New Standard Fishing Encyclopedia and International Angling Guide*. His good friend Curt Gowdy, an American sportscaster, longtime voice of the Boston Red Sox, and accomplished outdoorsman himself, called McClane "fishing's Renaissance man" and "the Compleat Angler" following Al's untimely death. McClane was one of the most respected anglers ever to stalk creatures with fins.

McClane also had Catskill Mountains roots, spending summers around Margaretville and frequenting the Catskill rivers, where the region's rich angling heritage was no mystery to him. As a *Field & Stream* essayist, McClane produced a "One for the Book" column

---

[1] The substance of this chapter is based upon Robert Hutton, personal communication, December 10, 2016 detailing correspondence between Ed Sens and A.J. McClane.

featuring fly patterns crafted by well-known tyers. In this role, McClane wrote to Ed Sens in December of 1947 asking Sens if he would contribute one of his "original patterns," noting: "Most of the nation's top-notch tiers are contributing to the column, and we would like to add your work to the list." Providing an example, McClane shared a Greig's Quill tied by Elizabeth Greig, a distinguished tyer Sens knew personally.

The two men exchanged letters on the matter, Sens using on an old mechanical typewriter with hand-written notes added. Sens submitted his Crane Fly, which McClane liked, but requested a size 8 Quill Gordon Nymph— the *Iron fraudator*, a Latin name a few of us older tyers may recall—that would photograph better. McClane added, "The flies are beautifully tied and certainly worthy of publication." And "I am compiling a thesaurus of fly patterns (in color) and would like to include both these flies in it. For the color work a larger nymph is essential. I'll keep the little one to take trout on."

Later, in 1953, McClane's *The Practical Fly Fisherman* incorporated several of Sens's nymph patterns, including the Quill Gordon. As noted in a prior chapter, McClane held Ed Sens in high regard, commenting that Sens' patterns "are fine references for the serious nymph fisherman." During these interactions, McClane also requested autobiographical information, which is expanded upon below.

Regarding Sens's father, Edmund August Sens (1875–1957), Ed noted that in his early days, Pop Sens fished the Esopus Creek, where he met Theodore Gordon, Herm Christian, Roy Steenrod, and Bob Whyte. Pop Sens extolled "the fishing ability and modesty of one Theodore Gordon," telling a young Edmund many stories about him. At the time when Sens responded to McClane, Theodore Gordon was not nearly as well known as he is today. John McDonald's 1947 book, *The Complete Fly Fisherman*, changed that. Not surprisingly Sens had a copy of McDonald's 1947 edition of *The Complete Flyfisherman* in which McDonald inscribed to young Sens, "For Ed Sens—the next T.G. with best wishes. John McDonald."[2]

---

[2] Robert Hutton, personal communication, December 16, 2016.

Ed Sens told McClane that his own "trout fishing career started on the banks of the Beaverkill at age 4," using worms. Pop Sens and he stayed at a boardinghouse run by John Ferdon known as the Hillside Summer Home. It was there that Ed met and befriended Winnie and Walt Dette. Then, in the early 1920s, Pop Sens purchased the farm along the Neversink where Sens developed his "intense fishing" passion.

Initially, Sens fished wet flies before trying dries. At age eight, he watched an individual he referred to as Judge Servin, a Neversink angler from Middletown, construct the first fly he ever saw tied. At that point, he took to tying himself, progressing from "raiding chicken coups" to tying for Jim Deren, when he worked in what he called "fly tyers' heaven." His fishing also progressed when Bob Whyte, an old friend of his father's, visited the farm. Whyte was a night fisher who used minnows, and it was Sens's job to keep Whyte supplied with bait, for which he was later given a Hardy rod. Sens wrote that his night fishing experiences with Whyte were "hair raising" involving "really enormous trout." Sens would go on to become a highly effective night fly fisher himself with his Giant Stone Fly.

Around the same time, Sens reported that Ed Hewitt, his neighbor downstream, introduced him to nymphs. While Pop Sens purchased nymphs from William Mills & Son, young Sens's interest improved by tying "easily hundreds of 'Who Done Its' trying to hit successful patterns without knowing what I was trying to imitate." Subsequently, Sens met a stage actor, fellow Jim Deren fly tyer, and nymph fisher named Ernie St. Clair who collected aquatic insects with Sens, keeping them in glass jars to examine. Over time, Sens developed the series of Catskill mayfly nymphs, caddis, and stonefly patterns that would be recognized as highly effective and precursors to patterns yet to come.

Ed Sens demonstrated tying his flies at various shows and invited McClane to come watch him at the Grand Central Palace. It was at such a show that Sens met renowned Pennsylvania wet-fly fisherman James Leisenring, where they discussed their craft. At a later date, Leisenring wrote to Sens with a formula for preserving collected insects, referring to Sens as the "Nymph Specialist."[3] J. Fred Geist's column "The Sportsmen's Corner," in the February 20th, 1948, issue of the White Plains *Journal News*, covered Sens's demonstration at this show in great detail.[4]

In a response to McClane, Sens wrote, "Up to this time salt water fishing has meant nothing to me" but goes on to say that while working at Abercrombie & Fitch, he was consistently dealing with striper fishermen who aroused his interest in saltwater angling. He told McClane that he had been fishing for stripers recently in a spot "exactly eleven minutes from my home in the Bronx," catching fish from six and a half to twenty-three pounds, and he invited McClane to join him.

It is truly thought provoking to ponder what Sens's influence on fly fishing might have been had he written about his own nymph patterns, as Schwiebert speculated he could have done. What would his Catskill legacy be now? Sens's Neversink research took place about the same time that Preston Jennings and Art Flick were doing theirs on other Catskill waters. What might have been, if only Edmund William Sens had put pen to paper?

---

[3] Robert Hutton, personal communication, December 21, 2016.
[4] Robert Hutton, personal communication, December 13, 2016.

Ed Sens—Select Fly Patterns

hese days the reader who desires additional detailed information about Ed Sens's fly dressings would need access to the 1951 edition of Ray Ovington's *How to Take Trout on Wet Flies and Nymphs* or his *Young Sportsman's Guide to Fly Tying*. As a point of interest, in Sens's personal copy of Freshet Press' 1974 reprint of *How to Take Trout on Wet Flies and Nymphs* =on the color plate facing page 107=Sens wrote, "Sorry, these are not my original nymph patterns, Ed Sens."[1] As was noted in a prior chapter, even before that in 1969 when Alfred A. Knoff published *Tactics on Trout* Ovington modified some of the Sens's patterns into "Ovington versions."

But it's well worth finding out about these early, innovative patterns. A. J. McClane in *The Practical Fly Fisherman* recommended "... the book by Ray Ovington, *How to Take Trout on Wet Flies and Nymphs*, which concerns in a large part the patterns of Ed Sens, are fine references for

---

[1] Robert Hutton, personal communication, November 23, 2016.

the serious nymph fisherman," because "it takes the patient research of an Art Flick or an Ed Sens to invent fishable nymphs."[2]

For the Sen's Quill Gordon Nymph, the *Iron fraudator* Sens provided McClane the pattern below.

Sens Quill Gordon Nymph:

Hook: Mustad 94836, size 14

Thread: Yellow Pearsall's Gossamer

Tail: Three wood duck whisps

Body: Pale muskrat fur, dyed light tan

Hackle: Pale blue dun dyed light tan, clipped on top

Wing pad: outside covert of coot wing trimmed to shape

For the Giant Stone Fly wet-fly dressing, which Schwiebert said "has seen excellent service as a night-fishing wet fly,"[3] the pattern below is the one published in Ray Ovington's 1969 *Tactics on Trout*.

Sens Giant Stone Fly:

Hook: Mustad R73-9671, 3X long, size 4

Thread: Brown

Tail: Mottled brown turkey feather

Rib: Yellow yarn

Body: Gray rabbit tied thick, with guard hairs extending out

Wings: Mottled brown turkey feather

Hackle: Long rusty dun

Angling literature offers slightly conflicting information on the dressing of the following two flies, with Ovington and A. J. McClane in one camp and

---

[2] A. J. McClane, *The Practical Fly Fisherman* (Englewood Cliffs, NJ: Prentice-Hall, 1975), p. 238.
[3] Ernest G. Schwiebert, *Matching the Hatch: A Practical Guide to Imitation of Insects Found on Eastern and Western Trout Waters* (New York: Macmillan, 1955), p. 128.

Ernest Schwiebert in another. Since my introduction to Sens was through Schwiebert, I've chosen to utilize his dressing, but with a proviso from McClane, who stressed the importance of "translucency" in the appearance of Sens's pupa, which might have been an important impetus for Gary LaFontaine in creating his Sparkle Pupas. I've also modified Schwiebert's dressing to include a floss underbody with a picked-out dubbed translucent overbody as described by Ovington. And in keeping with the spirit of these flies, for the Green Caddis I used a mix of LaFontaine olive Sparkle Yarn and Touch Dub. These are patterns that perhaps caused other tyers to see Sens as the man ahead of his time.

Dark Caddis Pupa:

Hook: #Mustad 9671, size 14

Thread: Black

Abdomen: Gray floss underbody, gray rabbit, picked out

Thorax: Brown seal dubbing

Legs: Dark brown partridge, tied long

Wing case: Thin mallard primary alongside

Green Caddis Pupa:

Hook: 14 Mustad 9671, size 14

Thread: Black

Abdomen: Apple-green floss underbody, olive Sparkle Yarn/ Touch Dub mix, picked out

Thorax: Brown seal dubbing

Legs: Long gray mallard fibers along body

Wing case: Thin mallard primary alongside

I still tie and fish these Sens patterns, which brought the creator such distinction, and they still account for their share of trout, especially his Giant Stone Fly on the Esopus Creek when big summer stoneflies are plastered along the rocks.

But for a Trout Fly

In 2017 upon completion of the Ed Sens's *Gazette* articles—which the four preceding chapters were based—good fortunate shone down on me earlier when I made contact with Bob Hutton, Ed Sens's son-in-law. Not only did Bob validate much of my research, but he also provided valuable insights and information not available elsewhere, so I owed Bob Hutton a huge debt of thanks and tried to repay his kindness when I introduced him to Robert Selb of the Classic Fly Fisherman in Landsdale, Pennsylvania. Hutton wanted to sell some of Ed Sens's fly-fishing gear, and I thought Selb could be an interested buyer.

These two gentlemen consummated a deal, and later that year, I ran into Bob Selb at a Catskill Fly Fishing Center and Museum Summerfest event, where I obtained several flies from Selb that were tied by the Ed Sens, including one of his prized Giant Stone Flies. Soon enough the day arrived when I would put a couple of Sens's flies to good use, if for nothing else than old times' sake.

Though it was very early autumn, on that September 24th day, it was hot, over ninety degrees and humid besides. The property around our house was littered with chocolate-colored dry leaves that sat over a dusty brown lawn. A very hot and rainless summer had just completed its cycle; our Catskill rivers were withering and warm. On the afternoon drive up to Frost Valley, there were swimmers and wet waders in Esopus Creek all about, but not a single angler anywhere. The DEC's Giant Ledge Trailhead overflowed with vehicles, almost as if the State of New York was offering a free give-away program, with endless folks waiting for their prize. Along the way, the Big Indian–Oliverea Valley popped with yellow, orange, and red colors that peppered the mountain forest. Sadly, the West Branch Neversink was seriously low, but cold enough and gin clear. On this outing, I planned to make a personal connection with Ed Sens.

Parked at Frost Valley YMCA's Western Model Forest Entrance, I fished the West Branch from the Iron Logging Bridge Pool upstream to just beyond the backside of White Pond, plus a few more yards. Initially, a size 12 Brown Bivisible tied by Ed Sens, was attached to the tag end of a 5X tippet. And it was cast on an Art Weiler Garrison 201 clone cane rod on legendry Catskill trout water, just about as Catskill as one can get.

On this warm, summerlike day, small wild brook trout came my way with relative ease. After catching a trout or two, I thought about not pushing my luck and removing Sens's dry fly, but I was in a groove, at the top of my game, so it remained on the end of the leader. In a fast-water run at the top of the Maintenance Barn Pool, a brown trout of some fifteen inches came off the bottom from nowhere, grabbing the dry fly and taking line. That instant really put me in my element, feeling boundless jubilation, until the 5X tippet broke, leaving that precious Sens's Brown Bivisible in the jaw of a trout.

At that moment, I had mixed emotions. Had the fly been lost on a poor back cast or without touching at least one trout, I would have been sick to my stomach. However, truth be told that Neversink wild brown enticed by Sens's fly just plain beat me. Plus, the fly had accounted for a half dozen Neversink trout before we parted company. Still, I pondered this situation a bit more, but then attached the only other Sens fly in my possession that day, a size 12 Fanwing Royal Coachman.

That particular dry fly accounted for seven additional wild trout: six more brookies up to nine inches long and one small wild brown. The last trout caught on that fly was a colorful nine-inch brookie that left the dry fly with very little material still lashed to the hook. At least I knew what it was and will treasure it in a special place among my cherished flies. I finished out the afternoon fishing one of my Elk Hair Stoneflies, picking up four more brook trout, including one a foot long before quitting.

It was a memorable day, for sure, one of the fishing highlights of 2017. It will be forever remembered for the flies used, the trout lost, and those caught. Ed Sens was gone, but never forgotten. Somewhere that evening, there was a Neversink brown trout swimming about with a Sens's dry fly stuck in its jaw. Perhaps a full half century passed since the last time a Neversink trout tasted the barb of an Ed Sens's tied fly. There are a few more of his creations still in my possession, none of which will ever be used on a trout stream again as long as I live.

Catskill Hollows

What is a mountain hollow and why might it be special to some? Dictionaries frequently define a mountain hollow as "an elongated lowland between ranges of mountains, hills, or other uplands, often having a river or stream running along the bottom." The Esopus Creek watershed upstream of New York City's Ashokan Reservoir is home to at least thirteen such hollows with creeks named after each including: Broadstreet, Fox, Hatchery, Jay Hand, Little Peck, Maltby, McKenley, Mine, Mink, Peck, Rochester, South, and Traver. Many, but not all of these, are located in the Catskill Forest Preserve, a regional area once thought to be "America's First Wilderness" before New York State Forest Preserves were created.

The Catskill Forest Preserve was initially established, with 33,894 acres set aside, by the New York State Legislature and Governor David Hill on May 15th, 1885. Since then, it has served as a gateway to a wilderness experience for an untold number of users. On April 15th, 1904, Governor Benjamin Odell signed a bill establishing the Catskill Park, which created an imaginary "blue line" encompassing four counties—Delaware, Greene, Sullivan, and Ulster—intended to delineate a boundary within which future forest preserve acquisitions should be prioritized. Originally, the park included ninety-thousand-plus acres of forest preserve; today, it's an area of over seven hundred thousand acres of public and private land. This entire region is rich in water resources, forests, mountain peaks—the tallest towering forty-one hundred and eighty feet —wildlife, recreational opportunities, natural beauty, and let us not forget wild trout. So much for a short history lesson and some baseline classifications.

So what's special about Catskill hollows?

For one thing, they can be secluded places where one can retreat from throngs of visitors invading these mountains. Often, they are deserted and devoid of human activities, plus internet and cell phone connections are frequently lacking. They tend to be nature's sanctuaries, time and again with thin chilly creeks, sheltered by a lush forest canopy, that serve as recruitment grounds for wild trout that eventually drop downstream into the Catskill rivers. They are outdoor churches, with their own special pews of decaying, collapsed trees and lichen-covered Ice-Aged granite. Choirs of songbirds chirp, small mammals rustle through the underbrush, while pesky gnats sometimes really annoy one's appreciation of the moment. The silence can be deafening, and the movement of tree leaves can sound like drumbeats. Typically, hollows can be cool and refreshing, even on the nastiest day summer has to offer. And frequently, they support their own unique histories, many times with clues to their past still to be discovered. Perhaps it's length of a rusty barbed wire, partially hidden and ready to trip bypassers, or maybe a fragmented stone foundation belonging to folks long since gone.

When wandering such a place, Catskill naturalist John Burroughs wrote in his essay "Speckled Trout," "The solitude was perfect, and I felt that strangeness and insignificance which the civilized man must always feel when opposing himself to such a vast scene of silence and wilderness."[1] Noted author Harry Middleton penned two fine works, *The Earth Is Enough* and *On the Spine of Time*, both stories of the Great Smoky Mountains, where numerous hollows are located. In the second book, he says, "In the mountains I first discovered the feel and significance of place, a solitude so rich that at times I felt sure I could feel the earth's pulse, the mountains' measured breathing."[2]

Most of these headwater hollows are home to little wild brook and brown trout, because rainbow trout often aren't able to ascend that far up into the watershed. How far into hollows wild Esopus Creek rainbows are encountered is often a function of natural barriers and flow conditions in the spring, when rainbow trout spawn. Plus, unlike wild brook and brown trout, rainbows tend to be more prone to wandering wherever their instincts lead them, and they don't stay put very often. While trout found in headwater hollows tend to be small, they are wild and the jewels of the Catskills.

During early spring months, I nymph the flows of these hollows, because their skinny water warms up the quickest, turning on both insects and trout. Often, the first few fish caught of every new trout season come from a mountain hollow, high-sticking weighted nymphs on a short leader. Hits are light, the fish tend to be small, but the moment frequently is memorable because the setting can be incomparable. Usually I call upon the services of an Epeorus Nymph, Martinez Black, or Casual Dress, weighted nymphs all that often are just what a hungry trout wants. However, come late summer and early autumn, when I'm escaping crowds, I return using a short, 7-foot 4-weight cane rod, 5X tippet, and small dry flies. Then most often I rely upon a size 16 Stimulator or Elk Hair Stonefly, because little stoneflies and annoying gnats are typically the only insects about. As I trek along the banks of these creeks, I'm always amazed when I observe a hidden trout dart

---

[1] John Burroughs, "Speckled Trout," in *In The Catskills: Selections from the Writings of John Burroughs*(Atlanta: Cherokee, 1990), p. 213.
[2] Harry Middleton, *On the Spine of Time: A Flyfisher's Journey among Mountain People, Streams and Trout* (Boulder, CO: Pruett, 1997), p. 7.

from waters below to intercept my fly. It's truly a science lesson learned firsthand, with nature my instructor.

There's a rich history associated with this mountain region. The Dutch, among the first Europeans to settle in the lush river basin, referred to the Catskills as "the blue mountains," due to a hazy blueness when seen from the Hudson River valley. According to the late Vera Van Steenberg Sickler, an Olive town historian, the Dutch also referred to the Esopus as the "Esopus Kil" and the "Grote Esopus," the Great Esopus. The region's Native Americans consisted of the Esopus Tribe of Lenape or Delaware Indians. They were gradually displaced by the onslaught of European settlers and a series of mid-1600 wars. The Native Americans referred to the area of today's Ashokan Reservoir as Ashocan, according to Vera Sickler. Her three little paperback booklets discussing the history of the Town of Olive are a treasure to be had, if one can find them. Then there are pages and pages of history retold in Alf Evers's monumental work, *The Catskills: From Wilderness to Woodstock*, the source of some of what follows. but also of much more.

Many of the Catskill hollows bear the names of landowners who once resided within their borders or of activities associated with each. Six hundred acres of Rochester Hollow once belonged to Colonel William R. Rochester, a former World War I US Army veteran. In 1915, he created this large estate after purchasing several small farms and lived there with his wife, Louise, until his death in 1932. On August 27th, 1951 the property was acquired by the New York State Department of Environmental Conservation, becoming part of the forest preserve, as a gift from Colonel Rochester's remarried wife, Mrs. Louise Howland. Some remains of the estate can still be found at the head of the old dirt road that once was connected to Rose Mountain Road.

Mink Hollow has a New York State Department of Environmental Conservation trail along the creek, consisting of a former dirt road that connected Lake Hill to the town of Hunter. This historic path dates back to the 1790s and was used to haul fur by Colonel William Edwards, who operated a large leather-tanning business in Tannersville. Reportedly, it was the main route for transporting hides to the Hudson

River's Saugerties port. In *The Catskills*, Alf Evers referred to it as "the Schoharie Road."[3]

Hatchery Hollow was once home to the early twentieth-century Big Indian Trout and Game Preserve. It was owned by James Cruickshank, a Scotsman who immigrated to New York City in the late 1800s, becoming a successful inventor. After selling patents to Otis Elevator, he relocated to Big Indian and in the early 1900s would advertise the sale of his trout in *Forest & Stream*.

South Hollow, which drains the flank of South Mountain in West Shokan is home to very special native brook trout. Located in close proximity is Maltby Hollow, where in 1880 Charles Maltby operated six charcoal kilns with upward of one hundred employees. That hollow became a small, self-contained mountain hamlet at its peak. Up in Shandaken, a Robert Fox once lived at the end of Fox Hollow, where a sign bore his name, And reportedly, Peck Hollow was home to the Peck family of laborers, quarryman, blacksmiths, chair factory workers, farmers, loggers, and millworkers.

Two Catskill hollows whose names were misconstrued over time include Broadstreet and McKenley Hollows. Reportedly, Broadstreet Hollow was originally named after Major General John Bradstreet (1714–1774), born in Nova Scotia and an officer in the British Army during King George's War, the French and Indian War, and Pontiac's Rebellion. Toward the end of his military career, he was stationed in Albany becoming influential in the Hudson River Valley. He tried to undo the Hardenbergh Patent in an attempt to secure large tracts of land for himself along the upper Delaware River. Evers dedicates a fair amount of ink to this individual. Bradstreet is buried at Trinity Church in New York City. At one time, a street sign for Broadstreet Hollow designated it as Bradstreet Hollow, but the sign was destroyed in an auto accident and replaced with a new sign that reads Broadstreet Hollow. It's not directly obvious what Major General Bradstreet's association was, if any, with this hollow.

---

[3] Alf Evers, *The Catskills: From Wilderness to Woodstock* (Garden City, NY: Doubleday, 1972), p. 236.

McKenley Hollow has two names associated with it also, according to street signs at its entrance: McKenley and McKinley. This always caused a bit of wonderment for me. The correct name is McKenley, referring to Dr. William H. McKenley (1864–1906), an African-American doctor who in 1902 assembled a one-hundred-acre Oliverea parcel he called McKenley Farm. His primary residence was in Manhattan, but he and his wife summered there. Dr. McKenley cofounded and became first president of the Afro-American Medical Society.[4]

As noted above, when fishing any of these hollows, the quarry often consists of small six-to-nine-inch wild trout. However, such is not always the case, especially early and late in the season, with spawning trout moving up into these waters. In over half a century of wandering the Catskills, some of my favorite little brooks have offered up a few rainbows and browns in the sixteen-to-twenty-plus-inch category. I recall one such afternoon on April 21st, 2009, a Tuesday following an eventful day at school.

I shared my middle-school math class with a student teacher, who came down with a severe cold and sore throat. Rather than remaining home to recover, this highly motivated individual came in, infecting the entire classroom with those nasty rhinosinusitis bacterial germs. Wanting to assist her, I resumed teaching while she stayed in the rear of the classroom, working on getting healthy again. After school that day, I sought fresh air to clear my lungs.

Though it had snowed the day before, late afternoon raindrops dripped from tree tops to the earth below, with a hostile spring chill in the air. Yet there was something invigorating about wandering through the forest under such conditions. Nature appeared in conflict, with buds blooming while snow covered the earth and a cold creek on the rise. I needed the outing, because I was a tad stressed. Since the start of 2009, I had more than my share of respiratory ailments and desperately wanted to avoid my student teacher's illness.

---

[4] Robert Burke Warren, "The McKenleys of Oliverea," *Woodstock Times*, March 6, 2020, p. 6.

Given recent snow and rain, I had no expectation of touching a single trout that afternoon. I was there to unwind, and unwind I did. A soft drizzle masked the setting while seductive sounds of the quick-moving stream and surrounding forest set me at ease. Polished round stones rolled underfoot, yet I remained upright; branches from overhanging deadfall reached out, trying to steal my weighted nymphs midair; aged fallen hemlock trees forced me to move about carefully; while those wild trout were totally uncooperative. Nature forced me to alter my pace, slow down, and experience the moment. Eventually, a smile filled my face as my inner being was at rest.

Now in tune with nature, I was pleasantly surprised when I missed a solid strike. I saw the fish's flash on the take and knew that was a good one, not a typical Traver Hollow trout. The creek's heavy flow and the time of year can pull some large trout up into it, out of the Ashokan Reservoir. Missing that fish sharpened my attention, though I'd detect only one other strike, but what a strike it was.

For whatever reason, I had forgotten my net and would sorely miss it. In a narrow rocky chute, a Lord's Prayer trout ate my Epeorus Nymph, quickly using the healthy flows to run past me, downstream through rushing water some hundred feet. I followed, stumbling along the way, but eventually beached an eighteen-inch, chrome-sided rainbow with the nymph firmly embedded in the corner of its lower jaw. Upon its release, I quit fishing, because this hollow had given me all it had to give. And I remembered what Jerry Kustich once said: "I will continue to follow the road that leads to water, because I believe—with all my heart—that everything really does make sense at the river's edge."[5]

Over many decades, these Catskill hollows have provided me great joy; they are my sanctuaries. Within them, I've often been able to address life's confrontations, finding a sense of peace, a feeling of being touched by our Creator as sunbeams filter their path through the overhead forest. Usually I end each outing saying the prayer of Divine Mercy and then have one cold beer acknowledging my good fortune.

---

[5] Jerry Kustich, *At the River's Edge: Lessons Learned in a Life of Fly Fishing* (Grand Island, NY: West River, 2001), p. 52.

Invasive Species—
Peck Hollow Brown Trout

T hough we might want to, who can forget Hurricane Irene? By the time it reached the Catskill region on August 28th, 2011, it had been downgraded to a tropical storm, but it still devasted Prattsville along the banks of Schoharie Creek, depositing over a foot of rain in about twelve hours' time. Folks thought the Gilboa Dam on New York City's Schoharie Reservoir could fail, causing untold amounts of human suffering and downstream destruction. When the waters eventually receded, New York City's Department of Environmental Protection would invest over a decade and some $400 million upgrading that water supply's infrastructure.

Closer to home, the USGS Coldbrook gage on the Esopus Creek reported a devastating flow of 75,850 cubic feet per second, while Allaben's USGS gage some ten miles upriver recorded a record flow of 29,300 cubic feet per second. Take a moment and think about a cubic foot per second. This would be a cube one foot long, one foot wide, and one foot high. How many of these could you hold? And imagine 29,300 of these, let alone 75,850 passing by you every second.

These were all-time high flows, never to be forgotten. My wife and I were without electricity for over a week as crews from all around the East Coast helped to restore power. And Governor Andrew Cuomo suspended many New York State Department of Environmental Conservation permitting laws and regulations, allowing almost anyone who owned a bulldozer to reconfigure stream banks at will, making straight roadways where Catskill waters flowed. These were hard times, and they stayed hard for a long time after a liquid hell rained down on the eastern Catskills, especially on the Schoharie and Esopus Creek watersheds.

The year following Hurricane Irene, the Esopus Creek watershed remained turbid for twelve long months, and its wild rainbow trout population seemed almost decimated. Thus, during 2012, I spent an inordinate amount of my time fishing other Catskill rivers, especially those that didn't suffer the same fate as the Esopus and Schoharie Creek watersheds. My Esopus wasn't fun to look at or to wander, but its many tributaries served as my saving grace, and most of them still carried a healthy stock of small wild trout.

September 20th found me up in Peck Hollow, following a rather chilly night resulting in the first woodstove fire of the early autumn as freeze warnings were issued. That morning, snow coated the Catskill peaks, while this mountain hollow brook was slightly elevated and lightly stained. Still, stealth was the day's watchword—sneakily roaming along a cold creek. The only other angler I encountered was a blue heron working hard to gather its meal.

Under a powder-blue sky, the air temperature never broke the forty-five-degree mark. I love fishing this time of year since our Catskill waters can be devoid of other human anglers. Gone are the meek of heart and dry-fly aficionados; our piscatorial numbers have dwindled to the very few fly fishers with true grit as another season winds down.

Using a weighted size 12 Flashback Hare's Ear Nymph on point with a size 12 Black Turkey dropper wet fly, I trod unhurriedly upstream, all the time hidden in a forest hollow. Along the way, I managed to touch two small, nine-inch silvery wild browns. That got me thinking.

How did these wild browns ever establish themselves in Peck Hollow? There's an impassable waterfall not too far upstream of the brook's junction with the Esopus Creek that even the wild rainbows cannot ascend.

Then, while walking the dirt road back to my vehicle, an ole-timer, some ten years my senior, pulled up alongside me. He was driving a rusted-out, beat-up, timeworn Jeep, partly held together with duct tape and dehydrated chewing gum. Courteously, he inquired about my fishing, because he was concerned about that blue heron stalking the creek's trout in the small water. I told him I had released a couple of little wild browns, but was confused by the origin of these trout, given the waterfalls downstream.

With a smile on his grizzly, wrinkled face and twinkle in those sharp eyes of his, he proceeded to tell me that years ago, he and his fishing buddy would catch brown trout in the mainstream Esopus and bring them back up into the hollow to release, hoping that they would take hold. Those browns established themselves and seem to be outcompeting the native brook trout in the lower section of this creek.

In this day and age of invasive species such as snakeheads, emerald ash borers, hogweed, and knotweed, not to mention yellow perch in brook trout ponds, I'm not endorsing this practice at all. However, I do think it's a cunning story, sort of along the lines of the fable of Dan Cahill and rainbow trout in Callicoon Creek back in the 1880s. And that got me thinking about the issues that fisheries like this face, especially following the hot, dry summer that just passed and hurricane Irene the year before.

On this particular outing, our local creeks were truly depleted, straining to support aquatic life. Birds and mammals that feed on fish have been picking them off during low-water conditions. With an impassable falls on this brook, this wild-trout population is self-sustaining through natural reproduction only, without added recruitment from other sources. Given climate change issues these days and their effects on nature, just maybe that ole-timer was ahead of his era doing us all a little favor.

The Dance

It rained hard Friday. Our local creeks were on the rise with the last 2013 Esopus Creek recreational water release scheduled for October 5th still to come. The Shandaken Tunnel was pumping out over eight hundred cubic feet of water per second and combined with last night's heavy rain, the Esopus was unfishable. However, the fresh influx of rainfall and today's warm October weather could have trout on the feed in tributaries. Thus I fished, even though it was the weekend; if nothing else, it gave me a chance to wander a local tributary that would soon close to all angling.

This hidden Catskill hollow was a kaleidoscope of autumn colors, with a fresh deposit of fallen leaves on the forest floor. In places, a wispy mist sat over the brook's surface, the result of warm mountain air that fingered a clear, cold Birch Creek. The brook was still a tad thin, but last night's rain helped rejuvenate it. According to the USGS gage downstream, the creek's flow had increased fourfold, but it was still a far cry from a bubbling, full-blown brook.

Sneaking up on the first small pool very deliberately, I watched nervous water resulting from trout chasing each other. I've witnessed this type premating dance before, often at White Pond, watching brook trout play around each other before they spawned in the days that followed. I believe this dance is nature's way of sexually stimulating wild trout as they get ready to build nests and drop eggs. Perhaps it's not really a dance per se, but trout battling each other to establish spawning dominance.

After observing this activity for several minutes and not seeing any trout redds, I slowly worked my way through this water, casting a size 16 Elk Hair Stonefly. That only spooked fish, including a good-sized dark male brown trout that would have nothing to do with me or my silly dry fly. As I continued on a half-mile upstream trek, and maybe more, the dry fly accounted for five juvenile browns, little wild trout that were not yet educated in the facts of life. And the small trout that I caught were fewer than half the number of fish that grabbed the barb of the fly, probably unable to pull it under.

I enjoy the experience of fishing over wild trout while trying to decipher the laws of nature that govern their existence, and these events caused me to ponder. I wondered if brown trout spawning activity starts earlier in small tributaries like this one than it might in mainstem rivers such as the Esopus. And do wild browns stop looking up at dry flies as spawning approaches, yet might they still intercept submerged flies that drift near unseen redds? Or is all this conjecture just about extremely nervous, late-season wild trout in skinny water?

I relocated once, deeper into this mountain hollow. As the afternoon wore on, more autumn leaves fell, and air temperatures rose to summerlike levels. That must have excited these trout, because I easily caught eight more wild browns before quitting. None of these were over nine inches long—most were dollar-bill length. Many of these fish came out of nowhere to take my dry fly in a transparent brook, totally hidden in the cracks and crevices of submerged underwater rocks, exploding to the stream's surface like little Polaris missiles.

This outing was both educational and confusing. Two seasons clashed. It looked like autumn, but felt like summer. And the color of this Catskill hollow was absolutely spectacular. As for the trout and the dance, it's what brown trout thankfully do every autumn, and I was there to observe it.

Gingrich and the Royal Coachman

first met Arnold Gingrich (1903–1976) in the fall of 1968, not in person, mind you, but on a second floor of Macy's in Menlo Park, New Jersey through one of his books. My future wife and I were wandering about the department store when the cover of his book *The Well-Tempered Angler* caught my eye. I knew nothing about Arnold Gingrich, but I picked it up, casually flipped through it, but then put it back down. I was a young wannabe trout fisher, and this book consisted of fly-fishing stories, rather than specifics and helpful hints on how to catch fish. Besides, at the time, I wasn't a dyed-in-the-wool fly fisher, still relying upon Mike's Glo Fluorescent Salmon Eggs to seduce the few hatchery trout that came my way.

Lois and I continued walking about Macy's, trying to kill time before a movie started in the attached mall. But eventually we found our way back to the stand with Gingrich's book, where Lois suggested I purchase it. What the heck, it cost less than six dollars, a sum even I could afford as a college student. Thus, I soon learned Gingrich was quite the writer and an excellent angler. He was also the founding editor and pub-lisher of *Esquire*, a distinguished author, journalist, nurturer of literacy, and avid fly fisher. Over the ensuing years, I'd read the *Well-Tempered Angler* from cover to cover several times and also read both his *Joys of Trout* and *Fishing in Print*. In fact, I've tried to read everything Arnold Gingrich ever wrote regarding fly fishing for trout. He edited *American Trout Fishing*, by Theodore Gordon and a Company of Anglers, a real classic and important angling literature. Gingrich became a genuine inspiration to me.

After moving to New York State, I exchanged letters with Arnold Gingrich, though it took Gingrich several months to respond to mine, writing that my letter "somehow got sidetracked." His letter has become a prized piece of correspondence that I've kept to this day. I wrote to him asking about his experiences fishing the Esopus Creek and upper Neversink. With regard to the Neversink, I was seeking to learn more about water to which I might be able to gain access—a river I had not fished since my early days. Gingrich responded regarding fishing both of these streams, but didn't have any suggestions concern-ing the Neversink, because his experiences were limited to once being a member of Edward R. Hewitt's Big Bend Club. However, he ended his letter with, "I envy your proximity to the Esopus, which was always my favorite stream, though I haven't seen it since Labor Day weekend of '56."[1]

When Gingrich fished the Esopus, he stayed at Dick Kahil's Rainbow Lodge in Mount Tremper, across from the Beaverkill, a main Esopus Creek tributary. And while staying there, Gingrich met Preston Jennings, who would occasionally demonstrate fly tying to lodge guests. Both men bonded. Plus, Gingrich's stays were not without some inter-esting sidebars, several of which were told to me by one of the late Dick Kahil's sons, Rick. Rick told me that one day, Gingrich fished the Beaverkill and afterward mentioned something to the effect that "I just came back from the pool up the road with all the big rocks and could

---

[1] Arnold Gingrich, personal communication, March 29, 1971.

see the most beautiful and plentiful rainbows just swimming peacefully and couldn't catch a damn one. How frustrating. I need a drink!" After that outing, the folks at Rainbow Lodge would forever call that spot Frustration Pool, though it was locally known as Flugers.

Rick went on to say that Arnold Gingrich used to pay him a quarter to walk his dog when he stayed at the lodge. However, the best story Rick told dealt with his being a young and aspiring businessman. Much to his father's chagrin, Rick attempted to sell Arnold Gingrich a few worms to fish with. Gingrich generously took the offer, but the senior Kahil made Rick return the money and tender a full apology. He said Gingrich gracefully accepted both.

In April of 1974, I helped our Trout Unlimited chapter organize its annual dinner fund-raiser and arranged for Arnold Gingrich to be the guest speaker. That was the first, last, and only time I ever met him in person, and he was kind enough to autograph copies of his books I owned. As noted previously, I've read *The Well-Tempered Angler* several times, and the second reading was an eye-opener for me. In came one June evening after flogging the Esopus Creek for days. In fact, Gingrich's March 29th, 1971, letter to me remarked, "I did get a kick out of hearing how those Isonychia nymphs (out of my chapter President Jennings for President) saved the day, or rather evening, for you that one night near Five Arch Bridge."

After I graduated from college and, my wife and I got married, we moved to upstate New York in June of 1970. I began a career working for International Business Machines, while that autumn, Lois started teaching elementary school in Marlboro, New York, a southeastern Ulster County hamlet. Up until our move, I had never fished the Esopus Creek, so fishing it was a totally new and exciting experience for me. Plus, just fifteen months earlier, I had sworn off the use of bait, using flies only henceforth. While I had read various books on the subject, I really didn't have much experience, especially when wild trout were involved. And I was never much of an entomologist—no Art Flick, for sure.

My initial Esopus Creek experiences found me wandering close to the Five Arches Bridge, because I didn't know the river well and commuted to explore it after work, driving up from Kingston. Those experiences were unpredictable, because they preceded the 1976 water-release legislation won by Catskill Waters, a seven-county coalition of conservationists. Until that regulation was enacted, anglers never knew if Esopus Creek flows would be fishable or high and muddy from Shandaken Tunnel diversions.

One June evening, I arrived to find the Esopus in good shape, with trout feeding as the evening wore on, but I never touched a fish. The next night, I returned again, resulting in the same experience. Fish were feeding once more, and I noticed plenty of fresh dark insect shucks along the river's edge. What could they be? That got me thinking on the drive back to our Kingston apartment, remembering something I read in *The Well-Tempered Angler*. Upon returning to the apartment, I immediately flipped through Gingrich's book, rereading "Preston Jennings for President—or, There is a Royal Coachman." In it, I found the secret. The bugs I encountered were "the nymph phase of the Royal Coachman," better known as *Isonychia* nymphs. Thus, a Hairwing Royal Coachman it would be when I revisited the Esopus.

For the third consecutive night, I returned to the Esopus, fishing the same section between Five Arches Bridge and the Trestle as I had done previously, but this time finally realizing *Isonychia* nymph shucks coated the creekside rocks. And I decided to follow Preston Jennings's advice, casting my little Orvis Superfine cane rod, just like Arnold Gingrich did, but with a Hairwing Royal Coachman attached to the tippet. Before the evening ended, I caught a dozen wild, dancing rainbows, including a sixteen-inch silver-sided fish immediately upstream of the now-gone U&D railroad trestle. Arnold Gingrich helped me salvage a victory following two consecutive hard-learned failures, and the Hairwing Royal Coachman has been a favorite dry fly ever since. Thank you, Arnold Gingrich and Preston Jennings!

Salvelinus fontinalis

Brook trout: there's a subject to which one could devote an entire book, as Charles Barker Bradford did in 1900, with Nick Karas eventually following suit ninety-seven years later. And recently, there's Bob Mallard's 2019 work, *Squaretail*. Squaretail, now there's a name that sounds magical. But a trout by any other name would be the same: brookie, speckled trout, eastern brook trout, red-spotted trout, native, brook char, and of course, "little salmon of the fountain." The fact of the matter is, brook trout aren't trout at all, but char. Scientifically, brook trout are a species of freshwater fish in the char genus *Salvelinus* of the salmon family Salmonidae. In his 1902 work *The Speckled Brook Trout*, Louis Rhead wrote, "The fact that this charming so-called trout of American waters is not a true *Salmo*, but a char, need not, it has well been said, occasion any sorrow to the angler or to the lover of the attractive fish, since all the members of this group of salmonids are noted not only for their beauty and grace, but also for their game qualities."[1] They are native to eastern North America and Canada, but have since been introduced elsewhere.

Historically, brook trout have been found from Georgia up through Canada along the Appalachian Mountains and as far west as eastern Minnesota and Iowa. However, climate change, water-quality issues, natural disasters, other environmental factors, plus encroachment by brown trout and other fish species have diminished their range. Case in point: as result of Hurricane Irene Catskills' impact, in 2011 Lake Cole overflowed along UC 47 allowing yellow perch and other warm-water fish to establish themselves in lower-elevation White Pond. White Pond harbored a wild brook trout fishery known to give up the occasional fish pushing the twenty-inch mark. I landed one that mea-sured nineteen inches in White Pond's heyday. However, such is no longer the case because yellow perch overran the small pond, destroy-ing what was once the crown jewel of Frost Valley YMCA brook trout angling, and perhaps the best brook trout fishery in all of the Catskill Mountains.

Brook trout don't fight nearly as fiercely as wild Esopus Creek rain-bows, nor are they as smart or challenging to seduce as wild Delaware River watershed browns, but if the Lord ever made a prettier fish than a wild brook trout, I haven't seen it yet. They are New York's only native stream trout and in 1975 were adopted as the state's official fish. These trout are found only in the cleanest, cold streams, ponds, and lakes, where they depend upon untainted gravel and springs for spawning, settings that tend to be aesthetically appealing. Often brilliantly col-ored, with a wormlike pattern across an olive back, yellow and blue spots broadside, an orange belly, chalk-white-edged fins, and some-times a tail that is set aflame, they are nature's perfect kaleidoscope.

One of the most fetching images of a brook trout wraps the cover of Ray Bergman's book *Trout*. And how about S. A. Kilbourne's leaping

---

[1] Louis Rhead, *The Speckled Brook Trout* (West Newbury, MA: Hand Thrown Books, 2013), p. 24.

brook trout that graced the cover of Orvis catalogues for decades? Plus let us not forget Homer Winslow's paintings of these beautiful fish. Yes, brook trout have caught the fancy and imagination of many. Stories of big brook trout have been attentively retold, such as Daniel Webster's monster brook trout, which he reportedly caught in 1827. It was a well-publicized fourteen-and-a-half-pound salter taken in a mill pond on Long Island's Carmans River.

While I've never caught anything close to that size, but being a Frost Valley fly-fishing club member for decades has provided me access to several miles of unstocked native brook trout water on both branches of the upper Neversink. At least one day of every trout season my vehicle will be parked at the end of a Denning dirt road, where I travel back in time to a Catskills probably as primitive today as it was a century ago. And I wander other places too, mostly New York State Forest Preserve lands open to the general public. The Catskill brookies I catch tend to be small, but they are wild. Eight-inch and nine-inch trout are good ones, and a rare foot-long fish is exceptional.

If we should ever bump into each other, I'm probably carrying an Art Weiler Garrison 201 clone, a 7-foot 4-weight cane stick. But sometimes I might be using an A. J. Thramer 6-foot 8-inch 3-weight F. E. Thomas Fairy clone, almost always tossing small dry flies. My favorites are tied on size 14 and 16 Mustad 94840 hooks, and include Hewitt's Brown Bivisible, a Yellow Stimulator, a Cinberg, and even my Elk Hair Stonefly, because small stoneflies reign supreme on these headwater flows.

I've wandered near and far in pursuit of wild brook trout, from my home in the Catskills south to New Jersey and north to Maine, plus in Shenandoah National Park in the Blue Ridge Mountains. In 2012, the Jersey Boys—longtime buddies, growing up together in the Garden State—and I fished Yellowstone National Park, where I caught an eighteen-inch brook trout in Blacktail Deer Lake, the largest fish I caught that trip. Plus, I've fished for them just about every month of the calendar year, but by far, my favorite time to pursue these fish in the Catskills is the summer. While many regional freestone rivers have warmed up and begun slipping away to slim, tepid images of themselves, I find great pleasure wandering the hemlock-lined, cool, clear flows of native brook trout streams. Not only is the water nippy, but often the mountain air above them is dry and some ten degrees cooler than at home, very comfortable in summer's most unrelenting heat. Two such summer outings come to mind, fresh from my angling dairy. I was younger then, and much more foolish in the things I did. Plus, I still taught school, wanting to utilize all my summer time off fully.

August 1st, 2006. We awoke early that day and it was already eighty degrees outside, so my wife and I decided to postpone a planned trip to Boston because the day's worst weather was still ahead of us. And so it was. The heat index would break one hundred and ten degrees, but off I went, with Catskill peaks engulfed in a soupy blue haze, as I traveled toward the mountains in search of cooler weather and wild brook trout.

I wandered the headwater stream with only hippers, minimal gear, and a plastic bottle of water. Quickly my clothes became thoroughly saturated in my own perspiration, even though a thin breeze over chilly water worked hard to mitigate the ugly heat. The clash of mountain air and cold water created a thick, ghoul-like mist that weighed heavily over the landscape. It was a scene similar to that of California's Golden Gate advection fog.

Not quite two hours elapsed before I quit. The day was more about fishing to prove it could be done under these conditions, rather than for any other reason. In all, a dozen and a half wild brook trout responded to my size 16 Yellow Stimulator. Most were midgets, but there were a few real monsters among them of six to seven inches in length. It turned out to be the most trout I caught on that watershed in a long time and maybe even more fish than I caught cumulatively there during the entire 2005 season. Small trout, but wild trout, they were making a nice comeback, following two years of historic floods. It was a good outing, worth every bit of my effort, for sure.

July 9, 2007. My wife and I spent the early part of the day spackling and painting our bedroom, plus helping a delivery truck unload new engineered flooring to redo an entire level of our house. Once those tasks were done, I shot down to Kingston to purchase additional supplies that the contractors required. On the drive back home, my Subaru's outside temperature gauge read almost one hundred degrees. Plus it was plenty humid outside also. Yet there was still a little time to spare, and I wanted to fish. I gathered my fly-fishing gear and drove up into the mountains, where the outside air temperature dropped some twenty degrees in roughly an hour's time.

I wasn't surprised by the change in air temperature, since some years patches of snow and ice can be observed there as late as Memorial Day. The afternoon's goal was to stay comfortable while avoiding bathers who might be cooling off in the cold creek. Our region had received plenty of rain in recent days, thus the brook held a good summer flow and was plenty chilly, with a sixty-four-degree water temperature. On the other hand, Esopus Creek which I had driven past on this journey, was elevated and muddy.

Once in the headwater stream, wearing hippers and minimal gear, I fished a size 16 Yellow Stimulator using my Art Weiler 7½-foot 39-5 Leonard clone, a 5-weight cane rod. This rod length offered good line control while keeping my leader and fly free from numerous exposed moss-covered rocks. This is a stream that Catskill naturalist John Burroughs wrote glowingly about, and whenever I wander it, I think of him. In fact, Burroughs wrote, "My eyes had never before beheld such beauty in a mountain stream. The water was almost as transparent as the air, —was, indeed, like liquid air; and as it lay in these wells and pits enveloped in shadow, or lit up by a chance ray of vertical sun, it was a perpetual feast to the eye."[2]

I'd wander several hundred yards, concealed under a dark hemlock forest, observing a few birds work the water hard as the odd caddis and Yellow Sally stonefly fluttered through the air. But it was late in the day, and soon this hidden mountain stream went to sleep, as they often do as soon when the sun disappears. By the time I quit, I had touched

---

[2] John Burroughs, "A Bed of Boughs," in *In The Catskills: Selections from the Writings of John Burroughs*(Atlanta: Cherokee, 1990), p. 226.

a half dozen dollar-bill-size dark brookies, fish with a distinctive blue sheen. The next day's weather called for hotter and steamier conditions yet, with thunderstorms in the forecast, but at least before fishing that afternoon I had secured enough materials to finish indoor home projects if I couldn't fish.

A while back, the Ashokan-Pepacton Watershed Chapter of Trout Unlimited formed a partnership with the Ashokan Watershed Stream Management Program, undertaking a Catskill Heritage Brook Trout Study in a Catskill hollow, a study in which I participated. With the necessary state permit to conduct this study, we caught several small wild brook trout, taking a tiny clip from each fish's caudal fin, but otherwise releasing the trout unharmed. We also retained the services of Spencer Bruce, PhD SUNY Albany, to analyze the DNA of all fin clippings. Dr. Bruce reported the following:

> Through Trout Unlimited's involvement and the use of current genetic techniques, we have demonstrated that the Brook Trout population [sampled] *(i)* does not exhibit signs of population structure within the sampled stretch, suggesting that landscape features within this watershed may be isolating the population from other distinct strains and/or stocked fish, *(ii)* That the [brook trout] population is genetically unique compared to other native New York strains, although it is more closely related to nearby native strains rather than fish from other geographically distinct regions, and *(iii)* that [the brook trout] exhibit no signs of mixing with stocked strains despite historical stocking in the wider region. This leads us to conclude that the [brook trout] population is composed of native fish likely uniquely suited to their regional habitat and should therefore be considered for the same level of protection as other "heritage" strain Brook Trout present in the Northeastern United States, in order to ensure their future viability and protect their novel genetic constitution.[3]

---

[3] Spencer Bruce, PhD, "Summary of Findings: Prepared for Ashokan-Pepacton Watershed Chapter of Trout Unlimited—Catskill Heritage Brook Trout Study."

Project participants were very excited with these findings and are working to ensure these fish will be protected in some future fashion.

Salvelinus fontinalis, the little salmon of the fountain, are native to the Catskills, present long before the first Europeans ever set foot in these mountains. Some consider these fish to be Ice Age relics. Since this chapter began with mention of Charles Bradford, let it now close it with reference to him once more. When queried about fishing, Bradford wrote the following regarding fishing for brook trout in *The Brook Trout and the Determined Angler*: "I think the best time is when you feel like it and can leave home and the business. The desire for fishing is like some diseases, in attacking a man with great severity without notice. It can be no more resisted than falling in love can be resisted, and like love, the best treatment is its gratification."[4] I can think of no better word to associate with *Salvelinus fontinalis* than love.

---

[4] Charles Baker Bradford, *The Brook Trout and the Determined Angler* (New York: Freshet Press, 1970), p. 27.

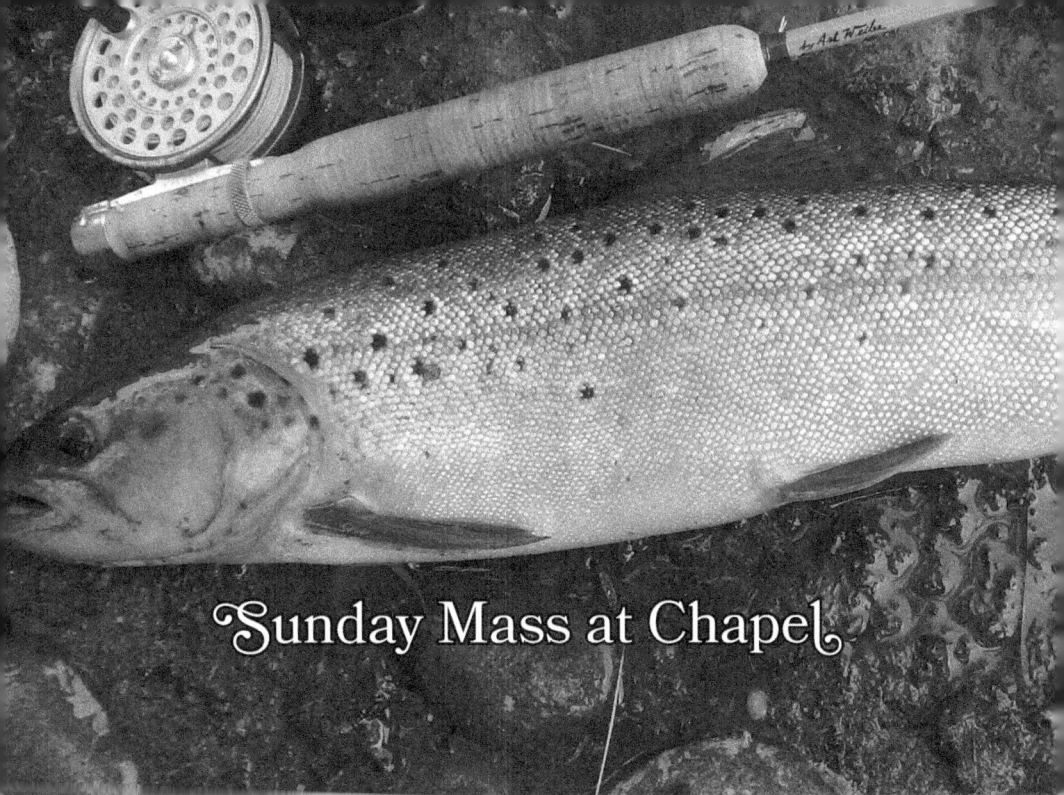

Sunday Mass at Chapel

Our local trout streams were low and warm, with water temperatures in the upper sixties and low seventies. Gravel bars sprouted up midstream where water once flowed. Little creeks I passed were fast becoming trickles, and in places, damp spots among exposed dry rocks. Air temperatures broke the ninety-degree mark, with humidity. And there was hardly a green blade of grass left in our front lawn. Under those conditions, who wants to fish, anyway? I did, that's who! This was summer brook trout weather, when mountain air is usually at least ten degrees cooler, with skinny clear flows that remain cold, offering a summer respite.

Typical of many summer Sundays, on June 26th, 2016, I attended morning Mass at the St. Augustine Chapel in West Shokan, a hamlet that T. Morris Longstreth called a "secluded haven of extraordinary charm" in his book *The Catskills*.[1] This small mission church was erected in 1952, an offspring of a late 1890s chapel funded by noted

[1] T. Morris Longstreth, *The Catskills* (Hensonville, NY: Black Dome Press Corp., 2003), p. 277.

artist Cecelia Wentworth, before New York City's Ashokan Reservoir swallowed up that building. My wife was away at an Adirondack quilt camp with friends. Thus, I had the day to waste by myself. After Mass, I continued heading west, through and over the mountains on my way to Frost Valley YMCA Camp and the East Branch Neversink.

Arriving at Frost Valley, I parked my truck and spent the entire afternoon near the New Road Hill Bridge. This is my wild brook trout Shangri-La. During the summer months, normally I fish it with a 3-weight or 4-weight cane rod, often tossing small dry flies such as Stimulators, Brown Bivisibles, Elk Hair Stoneflies, or Cinbergs. Occasionally, a small Black Gnat, Partridge and Orange, or Red Ibis wet-fly dropper is added a few inches below the dry. It's pleasant, easy fishing in pristine environments at their most enjoyable best, often negotiating gin-clear, chilly flows in old Catskill forests. Today, according to the USGS Claryville river gage, the East Branch was less than 50 percent of its seasonal flow, but it was still plenty cold.

Initially, I wandered a long section of classic Catskill water downstream of the bridge, lost in time and a hemlock forest. This section used to provide some unbelievable fishing for numerous small wild brook trout, but storms in recent years have changed all this. Now fishing here is only a thin shell of itself. Casting a size 16 Yellow Stimulator, I picked up a half dozen, or more, small brookies, nothing over seven inches long, in several hundred yards of water, fished hard. I also noticed mergansers diving in a pool upstream of me, with a fair amount of white excrement on streamside rocks, an outcome of nature's harsh reality and low flows. Those brook trout appeared to have been hunkered down with lips sealed tight.

Soon, I wandered favorite water upstream of the bridge. There was plenty of overhanging cover—fallen trees, undercut banks, ledge pools, and other homes for wild fish—in this section. Yet here, results were also disheartening—the fishing was slow and disappointing. With the lack of any bug life that afternoon, perhaps the trout were all hiding, given the low water and bright sunlight. Soon I changed to a size 16

Lime Trude, because this dry offers a smaller profile than a Stimulator and quickly caught my eleventh brook trout. Then the Neversink grew still on me.

As I continued to work my way upstream along a well-exposed gravel bank, a woody tree branch ate my Trude. Breaking the fly off, I retied my leader with 5X tippet material, but then added a small Yellow Stimulator again. Now I explored the upper end of what was locally known as Hewitt's Pool, and on the second cast there was an explosion under the dry fly. All hell broke loose as the surface of this small pool soon seethed with an animated brown trout. I guessed its size to be about sixteen or seventeen inches, which would be big for this headwater stream, but I was wrong.

Because it was a warm summer day, I had left my vest and landing net back in my truck, wandering with minimal gear. I had some tippet material and a few flies, but not much more. And I was fishing with my 7-foot 4-weight Art Weller Garrison 201 clone rod. Carefully, I moved the trout close to me several times, and several times it bolted away from me, back toward an undercut bank and fallen tree. In the low stream flows, this trout probably decided to stay the course in this small pool, not trying to run downriver. Still, I had all I could do to keep the brown away from submerged tree limbs.

Soon I drew it close to the rocky shore one last time, quickly dropping to my knees, grabbing the trout by its tail and flipping it up on the gravel bank. Not having my vest, I didn't have a tape measure with me, so I took out my wallet and laid dollar bills along its side. The fish's span exceeded three dollar-bill lengths, each of which is six-plus inches long. Excited and wishing for a more accurate measurement, I took out of a spool of tippet material laying monofilament line along the brown from its head to tail and then cutting it to length.

Pleased with this feat, I released the big brown after a couple quick photos and never took another cast, instead walking back to my parked truck. Luckily, I quickly realized I had left my wallet on the gravel bank in all the excitement, so I returned to retrieve it. Once at my truck, I measured the cut tippet material to be twenty and one-half inches long. What a great ending to a fine summer day: a big wild brown in skinny brook trout water on a light cane rod. Perhaps my chapel prayers had been answered.

TELLING ON THE TROUT

By
EDWARD RINGWOOD HEWITT

Hewitt, His Brown Bivisible, and Upper Neversink Tales[1]

lthough my college education was heavily grounded in engineering and mathematics, I always was a romantic history buff at heart. This feeling is based on the belief that it is difficult to appreciate the present without some sense of the past—where we've been and what has transpired before. When I was growing up in the Garden State, one of the first Catskill Rivers I ever wet a fly line in was the East Branch of the Neversink in the sleepy hamlet of Claryville, the very heart of the Charmed Circle, so designated in two 1969 *Outdoor Life* Cecil Heacox articles. It was love at first sight with Theodore Gordon's river. It appeared to be every bit of everything I had ever read concerning how a pristine Catskill wild-trout stream should look.

After graduating from college, moving to New York to begin a career, occasionally I stopped at the Darbees' fly shop during fishing trips to the Beaverkill and Willowemoc. In those early stages of my fly-fishing

---

[1] A version of this chapter appeared in the August 2012 *Gazette*, newsletter of the Catskill Fly Tyers Guild.

maturation, I never got overly excited about Harry's famous hackle, because I didn't know any better. However, I did take an interest in the used and out-of-print books that Elsie Darbee was able to acquire. Over time, I purchased several books from her, but by far my favorite two were Edward Ringwood Hewitt's *Telling on The Trout* and *Hewitt's Nymph Fly Fishing*. The second of the two is a small, thirty-one-page pamphlet with an original cover price tag of seventy-five cents. I bet this little green brochure is hard to find and worth a bit more these days.

Those books piqued my interest for two crucial reasons. As previously noted, one of the first Catskill rivers I ever fished was the Neversink, and I wanted to learn as much as I could about that legendary trout stream. Second, at the time, I was more of an avid nymph fisher than dry-fly angler, and there was very little written about nymph fishing available then. I discovered quite a bit from both books and back then felt that Ed Hewitt was an overlooked fly fisher. Yet he truly was a giant among Catskill anglers, a forward thinker, and a man clearly ahead of his time. This was before some of the fine books on Catskill angling history by the likes of Mac Francis, Mike Valla, and Ed Van Put were generally available.

Well, enough recollection, let's turn our attention to Mr. Hewitt and his Brown Bivisible. With the passage of time, I've just about worn the covers off my copy of *Telling on The Trout* reading the book over and over, continually delighted by each reread. I think it's fair to say that Hewitt gets credit for a few different notable fly patterns, including his hard-body nymphs, the Neversink Skater, and Brown Bivisible. While I never took a liking to his nymph patterns, I do tie and fish the two dry flies on a somewhat regular basis. Here's what the Dean of the Neversink wrote about his Bivisible in *Telling on The Trout*: "There is no fly which will catch as many trout as the Bi-Visible fly properly handled."[2] He went on to report that not all his fellow Anglers Club members agreed with him, but his personal experiences suggested otherwise.

---

[2] Edward Ringwood Hewitt, *Telling on the Trout* (New York: Charles Scribner's Sons, 1926), p. 61.

Hewitt credited the dry fly's enhanced ability to float in fast water while acting naturally in stream currents, plus its superior visibility due to the front white hackle band as the reasons for its trout-catching abilities. He added that the size of the dry fly and hackle were much more important considerations than wings and the body of a fly. He cited brown hackle as the most visible on the water, and the use of only hackle prevented this pattern from becoming waterlogged. He stated that his conclusions were based upon seasons of experimentation and testing different types of dry flies.

While the Brown Bivisible might be among today's forgotten fly patterns, that wasn't always the case. *McClane's Standard Fishing Encyclopedia* reported that it was a popular dry fly in the 1960s. Ed Van Put, in his wonderful book *Trout Fishing in the Catskills*, says that in the 1930s, "the Bivisible was possibly the most popular dry fly in the country."[3] Mike Valla, in his fine book *Tying Catskill-Style Dry Flies*, devotes a chapter to this celebrated pattern as one of the Catskill classics. Valla also provides excellent tying instructions with accompanying photographs.

However, long before I ever read anything by Hewitt, I read Ray Bergman's *Trout*. Bergman noted that seven dry-fly patterns could serve all his angling needs. Among these were three Bivisibles: a Blue, a Badger, and a Brown. I fished a Badger Bivisible, or Badger Spider as I called the fly back then, before I ever fished a Brown Bivisible, but I relied solely upon Bergman's description of the pattern as "being simply a Brown Palmer tied with a white face" to tie my Brown Bivisibles without consulting the recipe in the back of his book.[4] Bergman noted that while the Bivisible "didn't look like much . . . the trout liked it so well that they wore it out" before he caught all the fish he desired.[5] He concluded by stating that Bivisible flies "were the last word—the ultimate in dry flies."[6]

---

[3] Ed Van Put, *Trout Fishing in the Catskills* (New York: Skyhorse, 2007), p. 278.
[4] Ray Bergman, *Trout* (New York: Alfred A. Knopf, 1962), p. 184.
[5] Ibid.
[6] Ibid, p. 185.

When I finally read Hewitt's *Telling on The Trout*, I also relied heavily upon his description of the fly, which supported Bergman's instructions. Hewitt simply wrote " a Palmer-tied brown hackle on the head of which is wound a small wisp of white hackle" and failed to provide any additional detailed description of the pattern.[7] It's worth repeating that Hewitt wrote "dark colors are more visible to trout from below than light colors, and, therefore, take more fish under most conditions," touting its visibility as a main feature of the pattern.[8] He added, "This fly is by far the best of any I have yet seen for all species of trout and it is based on a sound physical principle."[9]

Every trout season, while wandering the East Branch of the Neversink, I often search its confines with a size 14 Brown Bivisible in honor and memory of the Dean of the Neversink. Brook trout relish the Bivisible these days as much as they did eighty years ago, when it was the dry fly that belonged in every angler's possession. And my longtime friend, the late Aaron Hirschhorn, told me that he used a size 16 Brown Bivisible on the Neversink below New York City's dam while pursuing its brown trout. Thus, this old Catskill dry fly still accounts for itself in the twenty-first century in an era of synthetics, foam-bodied flies, and genetically engineered hackle.

Edward R. Hewitt was born to a wealthy, established family, the grandson of Peter Cooper, an early American industrialist, inventor, politician, and philanthropist. Hewitt was Princeton graduate, engineer/chemist, inventor, author, naturalist, and fly fisher ahead of his time. Eventually, he became the patriarch of the Big Bend Club and caretaker of miles of water on the Neversink, an American pioneer of nymph fishing, an advocate of fine leaders and small flies, a forerunner of today's stream-improvements projects with his wooden-plank pool-digger dams, an experimenter with fish stockings, and fly fisher extraordinaire. For true Hewitt aficionados, I recommend picking up a copy of *Those Were the Days*, penned by the master of the Neversink.

---

[7] Hewitt, *Telling on the Trout*, p. 54.
[8] Ibid.
[9] Ibid.

There's not much fishing information included, but it does delve into Edward Ringwood Hewitt's life in great detail. In the book's final chapter Hewitt wrote, "I have also made many new types of flies for both trout and salmon fishing. One trout fly, which I introduced, although it was not entirely a new design, is almost the most popular fly in use today. It is the 'Bivisible,' so named because I could see it and the trout could see it."[10]

As I perused my book collection for material on this chapter, I realized perhaps it was time to reread *Telling on The Trout*, since there's a wealth of information packed between those covers. And so inspired by Edward Ringwood Hewitt, I acquired a copy of his *Days from Seventy Five to Ninety*. That was an enjoyable read also, providing insights into Hewitt's life and perhaps into some on the years that could lie ahead of me

Scanning through old angling logs, I noticed that I called upon the services of Hewitt's Brown Bivisible quite a bit during the summer of 2010. On the first day of summer, June 21st, I fished the East Branch of the Neversink. It had been a warm, dry spring, with Catskill streams evaporating, disappearing before our very eyes. Though the East Branch was low, it was also clear, chilly, and full of promise. The mountain air was cool and dry and brought the chatter of goldfinches; yellow buttercups and orange Indian paintbrush lined the side of the stone road where I parked. Rhododendrons were in full bloom; hemlocks stood tall.

Initially, I fished with a small Stimulator, touching some four dozen brook trout. Most were dollar-bill size and smaller, and the words of Leonard Wright, Jr., rang true: "Any Neversink brook trout that stretches to nine inches or better has to be considered a good one, and this has probably always been true."[11]

Then I relocated, heading downstream to a section of classic

---

[10] Edward Ringwood Hewitt, *Those Were the Days* (New York: Duell, Sloan and Pearce, 1943), p. 315.

[11] Leonard M. Wright, Jr., *Neversink: One Angler's Intense Exploration of a Trout River* (New York: Atlantic Monthly Press, 1991), p. 25.

Catskill water. Here, in old man Hewitt's memory, I attached a size 14 Brown Bivisible, and he smiled down from heaven on me. Before quitting, I caught another four dozen brook trout, including one that was a foot long. Without much effort at all, I touched nearly a century mark of small wild trout that day. When the Neversink fishes like this, it's not hard to do that; but for me, this river is more about history and place with the wild trout making it special.

On July 9th, I found my way to the East Branch Neversink's twin, the West Branch. The air was hot and sticky, but the river, while thin, was clear and cold. Once again I used minimal gear: some small fly boxes, leader, bottled water, and my digital camera. Entering the stream near the Eastern Model Forest entrance, I worked my way upstream, through what I call John Burroughs country, relying upon my A. J. Thramer F. E. Thomas Fairy clone 3-weight to drop a size 14 Brown Bivisible ahead of me. This section was well shaded and off the beaten track. Sunbeams struggled to break through the forest canopy, and the only sounds were from the warm breezes nudging tall evergreens and the muffled gurgle of trout water. Before quitting, I touched and released almost three dozen small wild trout, a couple of them little browns and a few brookies up to eight and nine inches in length.

Three days later, on July 12th, I was on to the West Branch Neversink again, because my wife was busy and I was free. Actually, I was there on the day before, too, but was chased off the water by thunderstorms. A healthy thunderstorm reinvigorates this stream during the summer months, at times offering some surprisingly good fishing. I explored the Western Model Forest entrance portion of the waters using my Weiler Garrison 201 clone 4-weight, and I alternated fishing a size 14 Brown Bivisible and small Letort Hopper. These two dry flies accounted for two dozen wild trout up to ten inches long, all brookies, except for a single brown. The best fish that I moved I never touched. It was a brook trout about a foot long that surprised me while I was watching nature, rather than my fly. It came out from an undercut bank, and I struck too hard leaving a Brown Bivisible attached to its jaw.

Then my buddy Joe David came north to spend a few days fishing the Catskills. On July 22nd, we ventured over to Shangri-La, fishing the East Branch of the Neversink. It had been a prolonged hot, dry summer and this headwater stream was definitely shrinking, but it was still plenty cold. Once again I relied upon my F. E. Thomas Fairy clone and a size 14 Brown Bivisible. We fished a number of different places long and hard, but at a leisurely pace. By the time we quit, some seven hours later, we had caught over one hundred and twenty-five small wild trout between us. On that outing, an eight-incher would have been a good fish.

Finally, days later, thunderstorms again rolled through the Catskills; the trout danced and so did I. The rain was much needed. After a morning Mass at the West Shokan chapel, I ventured through the mountains, finding my way to Frost Valley with a fresh supply of Brown Bivisibles and my 3-weight bamboo rod once again. I wandered several different sections of the East Branch to get a little taste of each, like dining at a buffet. However, as the day wore on, the sky filled in, and a light rain fell through the moist summer air. In years of fishing this stream, my best days have always been bluebird days, I've never done well there in foul weather. Nonetheless, by the time I quit, my Brown Bivisible had accounted for almost two dozen small wild brook trout. A couple of these were eight inches long and really fat, as if recent rainfall had provided them more food and places to eat.

So I am a longtime admirer of Edward R. Hewitt and his Brown Bivisible. These days, when I sometimes wander south to fish small Garden State wild-trout waters, I pass the former estate of the Hewitt family, Ringwood Manor, now a National Historic Landmark. Those were clearly the days.

Blue Ridge Mountains and a Shenandoah Angler's Log

y first visit to Shenandoah National Park (SNP) and its Blue Ridge Mountains happened in the midnineties with longtime buddies, the Jersey Boys: Joe David, John Julian, Rich Musolf, and Bill Nicol. Back then, we would plan late April and early May trips, hoping to entice Old Dominion wild brook trout to take our dry flies when most Catskill streams were still asleep and their fish wouldn't touch a juicy worm. Since those original Virginia jaunts, I've made numerous return trips, sometimes twice a year, but no longer executing the same routine and rarely with those Jersey Boys anymore.

Nowadays, I still fish Blue Ridge waters hard, hike its peaks and valleys, and trek along Skyline Drive, marveling at and photographing its splendid scenery. But now my wife and I might stay at Big Meadows Lodge, where we listen to others snore through paper-thin walls in cabins next to ours. However, just like old times, there has rarely been a bad experience in these Southern highlands.

Commenting on the one of the most famous features of these

mountains, the Natural Bridge, Thomas Jefferson wrote, "It is impossible for emotions arising from the sublime, to be felt beyond what they are here; so beautiful an arch, so elevated, so light, and springing as it were up to heaven, the rapture of the Spectator is really indescribable."[1] The Blue Ridge Mountains are old, some one billion to two-hundred and fifty million years old, and by several accounts among the oldest mountains in the world. They were created by an uplifting of the earth's tectonic plates and at their birth were reportedly among the tallest mountains on earth. The Blue Ridge extend some south six hundred and fifteen miles from Carlisle, Pennsylvania, into Georgia, a segment of the larger Appalachian Mountain range. These mountains are celebrated for their distinctive blue haze when seen from a distance, hence the name. Much of the geology of these mountains is composed of ancient granitic charnockite, metamorphosed volcanic formations, and sedimentary limestone. Their average elevation ranges from two thousand to four thousand feet, with a maximum height of sixty-six hundred and eighty-four feet at Mount Mitchell in North Carolina.

Some nine thousand years ago, Native Americans called these mountains home, perhaps drawn to the temperate climate and rolling, gentle character of the landscape. European setters followed, arriving over three hundred years ago. Centuries later on December 26th, 1935, Congress established the Shenandoah National Park. The first Civilian Conservation Corps unit, located there in May 1933, played a major role in the park's construction with President Franklin Delano Roosevelt formally opening the park on July 3rd, 1936.

While the mountains in the park remain richly forested, in recent years, the hemlock woolly adelgid, an invasive insect from East Asia that feeds by sucking sap from hemlock and spruce trees, has wreaked havoc on the countryside. Yet numerous species of mammals still make these mountains home, the largest among them black bears and white-tailed deer. And then there is the colorful native brook trout, the beautiful *Salvelinus fontinalis*. As Dr. Paul R. Needham noted in *Trout*

---

[1] Thomas Jefferson, *Notes on the State of Virginia*, ed. William Peden (Chapel Hill: University of North Carolina press, 1955), p. 25.

Streams, "The Eastern brook trout, *Salvelinus fontinalis,* is one of our most prized game fishes. Not only for its very beautiful coloration, gaminess, and edible qualities is this fish a favorite with anglers, but also because its home is in our most picturesque streams."[2]

I never ventured to SNP without Harry Murray's *Trout Fishing in the Shenandoah National Park.* Using this little paperback reference, I've explored many of the park's waters including Brokenback Run, Hogcamp Branch, Hughes River, Jeremy's Run, both branches of Naked Creek, Paine Run, Piney River, Rapidan River, Rose River, Thornton River, plus White Oak Canyon and many others in Murray's book and some not mentioned. In recent years, I even branched out into nearby George Washington National Forest highland creeks. There is a wealth of native brook trout waters to be discovered, if one only takes the time to do it. There are many favorite memories and waters that come to mind, and not all of these recollections have to do with fishing. However, what follows are some of those angling adventures from a Shenandoah angler's log. The angling log recollections below are not meant to be boastful or braggadocious, but rather shed light on a great Blue Ridge brook trout fishery that might be a thing of the past.

In the early days, the Jersey Boys and I did most of our fishing by wandering down into a hollow from Skyline Drive, a scenic roadway that traverses one hundred and five miles of the park. Frequently, we'd travel the road from Front Royal south toward milepost sixty-five at the Swift River Gap and US 33. Somewhere along the way, we'd park at a scenic pullout, hiking a trail into a recess below that bordered a small creek. Shenandoah National Park offers a multitude of outdoor activities attracting over one million visitors yearly who take pleasure in hiking, camping, horseback riding, sightseeing, stargazing, watching wildlife, or fishing like us. On fair-weather days, many of the Skyline Drive parking areas overflowed with vehicles displaying license plates from various other states, plus there were numerous visitors from

---

[2] Paul R. Needham, *Trout Streams: Conditions That Determine Their Productivity and Suggestions for Stream and Lake Management* (New York: Winchester Press, 1969), p. 23.

other countries. Such is the draw of this park and the Blue Rudge Mountains. However, our prime objective was always fly fishing for brook trout while enjoying each other's companionship.

Prior to 2004, my angling logs lack detail—not much more than one-line entries. Thus, for most of those early years, I rely mainly on the gray matter above my shoulders, home to the few remaining memory cells still in my possession. Those original trips were usually made in a Jersey Boy foursome, often composed of Joe David, Rich Musolf, John Julian, and me, but occasionally Bill Nicol and sometimes Glenn Debrosky—The Polish Prince—would swap in or add on.

My initial trip included Joe, Rich, and John in early May 1995. Assembled at Joe's Maryland home the night before, at daybreak we assaulted the national park for a spring weekend. That first day we four fished the Rose River. For John and me this was our inaugural trip, still wet behind the ears. However, Joe and Rich had fished the Rose before. As we all hiked up a wooded trail, Joe and Rich suggested that John and I drop off and start fishing the lower section. We obliged not knowing our buddies were heading upriver to what they thought was the best water. It turned out that John and I caught close to a hundred brook trout collectively, while our buddies struggled to catch a dozen fish each. As angler, author, and humorist Ed Zern noted in "The Ethics, Perhaps, of Fly Fishing," "Fly-fishing, or any other sport fishing, is an end in itself and not a game or competition among fishermen,"[3] especially with friends. Lesson learned!

On the second day in 1995 we wandered the Rapidan, which with time grew to captivate my imagination. In 1996, we returned again in early May to fish the Brokenback, Hughes, and the Rose once more with some seventy-five brook trout accounted for on my part during that trip. But the 1996 Hughes River outing ended on a very hot, very humid, ninety-degree day, and unfortunately, I wore waders while forgetting to bring water. John had a particularly good day catching over half a century's worth of brook trout, and thus he was the last man back

---

[3] Ed Zern, "The Ethics, Perhaps, of Fly Fishing" in *The Quotable Fisherman*, ed. Nick Lyons (New York: Lyons Press, 1988), p. 151.

to our rendezvous, while I sweated something fierce and quit early. Dehydrated and returning to the parked vehicle first, with nothing else to drink, I started drinking cold beers to quench my thirst. By the time John returned, I was three sheets to the wind. Oddly enough, the same thing had happened to John on a different trip, when he fished the Hughes and forgot water. What comes around often goes around.

In May 1997, The Polish Prince joined us Jersey Boys. We fished the Hughes the first day and Jeremy's Run the second. Collectively, both days provided me close to ninety brook trout for the trip. However, a notable event occurred that first day. We all agreed to rendezvous at a predetermined time, but The Polish Prince didn't have a watch and leisurely fished the day away. The four of us returned, and hours went by, with Glenn never showing up. We thought about asking park rangers to search for the Prince, when out of the blue, he appeared. He told us he didn't have a watch and "was catching fish." Earlier, we all were a tad displeased with his absence, but no one said a word to Glenn. I'm not sure if we were just happy to see the Prince or afraid to confront him, but either way, that ended the day's fishing.

In early May of 1998, we fished Jeremey's Run first and then Brokenback the second day. I caught over one hundred brookies in Jeremey's and totaled over one hundred and fifty small wild fish for the weekend. Brook trout fishing in SNP was that good in those early days, but then there was a several-year void in trips on my part.

My angling logs contain more detail for trips that occurred between 2004 and 2011. In 2004 Joe, Rich, John, and I split time fishing Jeremey's Run and the Piney on the first day and the Rose half of the second day. On May 1st, Rich and I dropped some twelve hundred feet in elevation along Jeremey's Run, and while fishing mostly a size 16 Lime Trude, I touched over sixty small brook trout. That day, the four of us released some two hundred and fifty brookies, with Joe and John catching a couple of foot-long trout. It rained hard that night, and the next day, the mountain air was heavy and moist, almost like breathing liquid oxygen. We fished an elevated Rose River, where I managed to catch only five more brookies while exhausting my Lime Trude supply.

Sadly, I have no log entries for 2005 through 2008, because life placed new demands upon me.

In 2009 Joe, John, Bill, and I fished the park together. On May 2nd, Joe and I dropped some eleven hundred feet in elevation along Jeremy's Run. Flogging the little brook long and hard with a size 16 Mr. Rapidan, I caught over ninety brook trout, most in the four-to-six-inch range, but wild trout all. That night, it rained hard again. On half-a-day Sunday, Joe and I fished an elevated Piney, where another dozen brookies, a tad larger than the day before, came to hand. Unfortunately, when Bill fished the Piney the day before us, he was bitten by a tick and came down with Lyme disease two weeks later.

In 2010, Rich and I drove to Maryland, spending the night at Joe's house. On April 30th, the two of us fished a crowded Rose River, flip-flopping around each other and other anglers. It appeared that the secrets of Shenandoah National Park brook trout fishing had finally gotten out. Alternating between nymphs and dry flies, I touched twenty decent brook trout that day, but that night, the air temperature never got below eighty-five degrees. The next day, we fished the Conway River, where the air was heavy and warm, and unknowingly, we wandered this heavily forested river behind another fly fisher. There, I caught only one brook trout, which took a size 14 Conover. Later that day, though, we fished the Rapidan, and I ended this two-day journey with a total of four dozen brook trout. That evening, after showers and a couple cold beers, we enjoyed dinner with Joe and John, who had fished other parts of the park.

In 2011, Rich and I ventured to Virginia by ourselves, where streams were flowing over their banks and fishing was poor. On April 29th, we fished Jeremy's Run, where I managed an all-time daily low of thirteen brook trout. The next day, we fished the Rapidan and White Oak Canyon, where the parking lot was packed with sightseers drawn by the roaring waterfalls. That was the worst fishing day I've ever experienced in the park, catching but one small brook trout. The weekend ended with fourteen brookies, some fat and well fed, mostly taken on nymphs, but the fewest number of trout I ever caught in the Blue Ridge.

The signs of a fishery in decline were clear to me, or at the very least, I had lost my way. However, that weekend, thanks to Rich, I also secured my National Park Senior Pass for the bargain lifetime fee of ten dollars.

There are other memories, for sure, but mostly the Jersey Boys and I recall long hikes back up to Skyline Drive in warm weather wearing waders and burdened with fishing gear, hikes that exhausted us at the day's conclusion. A cold beer was always a welcome reward for the end of such an outing, when catching upward of thirty or more small wild brook trout was the norm for the day. And who can forget the great times we shared at day's end, eating run-of-the-mill meals at economy seasonal establishments while enjoying each other's company. Our smiles and laughter made the food taste better, especially after long, hot hikes down from and up to Skyline Drive in waders during early summer heat spells.

For my part, all this ended in 2012, when I started making annual Virginia trips, sometimes two a year, with my wife, who visited her sister while I did my own thing fishing the park. Nevertheless, in the spring of 2018, we Jersey Boys attempted a reunion of sorts, but it rained hard, the rivers flooded, while the roads and the park were closed. So we aborted that attempt. I hope someday we can meet again, revisiting a national park filled with many fond memories.

In early March of 2018, my wife and I made a journey so she could help her younger sister recover from knee surgery. Despite very cold temperatures and snow, I was left to my own devices to fish. However, prior to the trip, my yearly physical and other medical tests resulted in my primary care physician informing me that I had severe aortic stenosis, though I never exhibited any symptoms of this disease. I remember his call like it happened yesterday. He told me that I needed to see a cardiologist as soon as possible, and in the meantime, if I experienced any chest pain or fainted, I should check myself into an emergency room right away.

Well, I didn't even know what aortic stenosis was, nor had I ever seen a cardiologist in my life. Before making that trip south, I tried scheduling an appointment with a heart doctor, but the closest date available was seven weeks out. Seven weeks! And check into a hospital if I have any chest pain? Imagine that. If I had a minor health issue such as a sinus infection or toothache, chances were excellent I could get needed medical assistance the same day I called.

Even so, we made the trip with that diagnosis hanging over my head, and I fished as usual, plus visited Harry Murray's Edinburg fly shop. However, unlike prior trips, when I hiked down into the depths of a mountain hollow, I fished only in the general vicinity of my vehicle. Despite snow and ice that caused Sky Line Drive treetops to glisten, I caught a few brook trout in the Thornton and in Pitt Spring in George Washington National Park on a Martinez Black weighted nymph and never worried about medical matters. However, in all my Shenandoah visits, that was the first time I recall not catching a single trout on a dry fly.

In December 2019, thirteen months after my heart operation, we made another trip south when Lois's younger sister required surgery again. And once again it was a cold, wintery trip with snow. I fished the East Branch of Naked Creek at the base of the Blue Ridge Mountains and using a weighted Martinez Black on point, plus a Pink Squirrel dropper, catching a double-digit number of native brook trout up to nine inches long. But once again, it was a trip where not a single trout succumbed to a dry fly. Yet it still was a most memorable venture.

And then there's my fondness for Virginia's Rapidan and its rich history. Reportedly, the name was derived from that of England's Queen Anne and the rapids in the river—the stream was originally called the Rapid Ann River. The river corridor was the site of several Civil War conflicts, including the Battle of the Wilderness in May 1864, the first time Ulysses S. Grant faced off against Robert E. Lee. Plus, it was once home to a fishing camp for Herbert Hoover, our thirty-first president. On May 7th, 2012, my wife and I hiked into Camp Hoover, which the former president called Rapidan Camp. We called that venture a "date day."

That morning, the fog along Skyline Drive was thick as pea soup, so we hiked into the camp from the base of the Blue Ridge Mountain, entering through Rapidan Wildlife Management Area, making it a six-mile-plus round trip. For the entire journey we followed the gorgeous, clear, free-flowing Rapidan River. We found Hoover's camp situated where Mill Prong and Laurel Prong meet to form the Rapidan. The camp consisted of thirteen rustic cabins and other stone structures, with various gardens and waterfalls. The Hoovers stayed in the Brown House, while England's prime minster, Ramsey MacDonald, and other dignitaries, would stay in the Prime Minister cabin. Plus, President Hoover even had his own trout pool built. In his book, *Fishing for Fun and to Wash Your Soul*, Herbert Hoover wrote, "Next to prayer, fishing is the most personal relationship of man; and of more importance, everyone concedes that the fish will not bite in the presence of the public, including newspapermen."[4]

The Hoovers purchased this one-hundred-and-sixty-four-acre parcel in 1929 as a retreat from Washington, DC, politics, and the camp was constructed by US Marines. The Hoovers entertained quite the list of who's who and other political notables at their camp, while the Secret Service maintained an on-site office. In 1932, the Hoovers donated Rapidan Camp to the Commonwealth of Virginia for use as a presidential summer retreat. And in December of 1935, it became part of Shenandoah National Park. Later on our 2012 date day, I fished the Rapidan using a size 12 Mr. Rapidan dry fly, catching a handful of presidential brook trout, a memory I dearly cherish.

As noted, many an SNP outing was spent wandering the Rapidan River, but of all the park's waters, this one always seems to treat me with total disregard, because its wild trout can be hard to come by, at least for me. However, in recent times, I don't catch nearly as many brook trout anywhere in Shenandoah National Park as I once did. I don't know if that's the result of more angling pressure, or if it's climate change or other weather factors, such as dry summers, or if it's just cyclic, but catching is not as good as it once was, at least for me. I used to enjoy catching twenty, thirty, forty, or fifty brook trout and sometimes

---

[4] Herbert Hoover, *Fishing for Fun and to Wash Your Soul* (New York: Random House, 1963), p. 76.

more on daily outings with the Jersey Boys in those early days, all on a dry fly. One long day in 1998, I even caught over one hundred brook trout in Jeremy's Run. The vast majority of these trout were well under six inches long, but they were native trout and willing to take my dry fly. Now, if I catch a dozen or so trout over the entire trip, I seem to be doing well, but the scenery, history, and allure of this national park still exert a strong pull for me. As Harry Middleton declared in *On the Spine of Time*,

> It is not how many experiences we pile up in our lifetime, but what we make of them, how they mix with the blood and memory, how they enrich our lives. Mountains and trout streams sustain me, are the handles through which I have glimpsed the slight and the immeasurable, the vast and the small. Being among them is never disappointing, even when there are no fish. For there is always sensation, so deeply satisfying, of belonging, of being genuinely connected.[5]

This particular chapter was longer than others in this volume, but it covered a quarter century of Blue Ridge Mountain fishing, during which a full head of brown hair disappeared, with a gray beard now the majority of the fuzz still on my head. It began with the discovery of an interesting natural resource and continued through adventures that included trips to assist family members recovering from surgery on worn-out body parts. I firmly believe those early days in the midnineties, extending into the new millennium, were the golden days of fishing in Shenandoah National Park, at least for me. But I can't complain one iota, because I'm on borrowed time, having beaten as serious heart issue I never knew I had. As for these mountains and their hidden treasures, they still remain as inviting these days as when the first Native Americans arrived.

Because current Blue Ridge Mountain visits are now made solely

---

[5] Harry Middleton, *On the Spine of Time: A Flyfisher's Journey among Mountain People, Streams and Trout* (Boulder, CO: Pruett, 1997), p. 62.

with my wife, and I'm always fishing alone, as age has assailed my body, I take more precautions. The park covers three hundred and eleven square miles, which would make it difficult for my wife to find me should something happen. And these days, I make as many angling trips from the base of the Blue Ridge Mountains as I did years ago dropping down from Skyline Drive. Often, I find many of these locations to be in stark contrast to what they were. There now are well-manicured horse farms with white picket fences and big Southern Gothic homes and large horse barns, the homes of Southern aristocrats, for sure. Other places are draped with Confederate flags, with abandoned, worn-out vehicles and broken-down wooden shacks and poorly painted "Keep Out" signs in plain view. These folks appear to be struggling just to get by. Yet no matter where one travels, often in the not too far distance sits the majestic forested base of the Blue Ridge Mountains, frequently shrouded in a thick pea-soup fog. Online, I once read, "Brook trout are God's way of saying everything is going to be all right," and so it continues to be.

Winter's Window[1]

Roughly a decade after the conclusion of the last millennium, I began winter fly fishing for trout in earnest. Many years disappeared since I last fly fished for steelhead, lake-run browns, and Pacific salmon in Great Lake tributaries during cold winter months, but wild stream-bred winter trout, that's a totally different story. And so is Northeast winter fly fishing. It can be unlike any other trout fishing in freestone and tailwater rivers, and totally different than trout fishing in ponds and lakes under warmer conditions. Following the cold, dark days of the seasonal holidays and New Year's, this type of angling can be just what the doctor ordered, a sure-fire way to address the winter shack nasties. But the window of opportunity on any given day can be very short and the number of fishable days in any month very limited. You almost need to be retired to fish on twenty-four hours' notice and a single good weather forecast, because that's all a month like February might afford.

---

[1] A version of this chapter appeared in the January 2018 *Gazette*, newsletter of the Catskill Fly Tyers Guild.

At the end of 2012, I seriously took up the pursuit of winter trout fishing, aspiring to catch at least one trout on a fly every month of the year. This opened a whole new diverse angling perspective, while acquiring a few idiosyncrasies along the way. These chilly escapades offered a fresh set of stimuli, perhaps the most important being the opportunity to interact with nature again after endless days sitting home, tying flies by a warm woodstove. There is nothing as surreal and serene as the deafening sounds of falling snow, mixed with the gurgle of a trout brook half choked with ice. Often I'm the only angler about, and just hearing a junco or seeing a blue jay might be the day's highlight, with a struggling Little Black Stonefly a real bonus. Initially, I fished Catskill streams still open to angling and the Farmington in Connecticut, but soon learned to head south—south to the Garden State, where the climate might be a tad warmer and the streams ice free.

A half dozen flies will do just fine during winter. Mostly I nymph on a short, tight line, often with only the leader touching the water. My favorite patterns include three weighted nymphs: a size 10 Casual Dress, a size 10 Martinez Black, and a size 14 Pink Squirrel, the last solely used as a dropper. I like generic patterns that represent diverse food forms trout feed on. I'm also very fond of fishing a size 8 Red Butt Conehead Woolly Bugger or a size 6 Slumpbuster if real depth is required to put a fly in front of a trout's nose.

Typically, the trouts' sluggish metabolisms mean they don't move about much in cold water. My favorite places to drown flies are pockets and small plunge pools, which usually remain at least partially ice free. Once in a while, I might need a dry fly, and then I rely upon an Adams or Dorato Hare's Ear in sizes 18 or 20. This time of year, an angler might only encounter a few midges, tiny Olives, or Early Black Stoneflies. Thus, boxes of flies aren't necessary and only weigh one down.

Timing is everything in winter fishing. Air temperature and time of day tend to be critical. Normally, the best fishing occurs a few hours after sunlight first touches the water, up to about 1:00 PM, maybe two o'clock. My experience has found that freestones streams shut down for the day once shade creeps back over them. The window of opportunity is very narrow, so I try not to waste time changing flies, especially when there are no hatches to imitate. On days when the terrain is snow covered or the brooks lined with ice, I've experienced my greatest success fishing early, before snowmelt can affect the water, and that's why I also prefer days with air temperatures around forty degrees or only slightly higher.

Snowmelt affects the stream in several ways, depending upon the percentage of the stream's flow volume it influences. First, it depresses already cold stream temperatures, thus further dampening a fish's metabolism. Large amounts of snowmelt will also raise the stream's volume and flow, making it more difficult to place a fly in front of lethargic trout. But I think the most important factor is that snowmelt can change the water's chemistry. There have been several scientific papers written on the topic of snowmelt and episodic acidification, that is, a lowering of the water's pH. I believe this can depress trout feeding and cause fish mortality, especially to young of the-year trout in some cases. Two such snowmelt incidents, of numerous ones I've experienced, are cited below.

The most significant incident occurred while I taught middle school math while participating in the Trout in the Classroom (TIC) program. The science teacher and I each had our own TIC fish tanks and tried to vary conditions in each. One year, she used bottled water while my tank used stream water from an adjacent brook along school property, which also supported trout. When TIC fish reach a certain size, roughly 50 percent of the water in the tank must be replaced on at least a weekly basis to remove fish waste while addressing potential pH issues.

One warm winter day during winter break with snow along the brook, I took replacement water needed from the brook, recycling half the fifty-five gallons in the tank. The brook contained substantial recent snowmelt, but sadly I didn't give that matter any thought. The very next day, my TIC tank suffered over a 50 percent fish mortality rate. The significant drop in pH caused by the creek's replacement water was the cause. The science teacher's trout were fine.

Then there was a time years later when a winter day was forecast to reach sixty degrees, and I fished a little brook containing wild rainbows. Fortunately, that morning I started fishing the ice-lined brook, with snow-covered banks, by 9:00 AM and quickly caught almost a dozen small wild rainbows using a Casual Dress Nymph. However, after 10:30 AM I never detected another hit. By the time I quit air temperatures had risen over fifty degrees and were climbing under a bright, sunny sky. Rivulets of snowmelt ran all about the landscape and into the trout stream. Snowmelt causes streams to take on an aqua tint, so it's easily recognizable. Later that evening, a USGS stream gage revealed that brook's volume had swiftly doubled that morning.

Winter angling is unique and often special in its own way. I look forward to these days, though often a calendar month might not offer up many opportunities. When snowmelt is a factor, I've learned to examine fly fishing through an entirely different lens, one not used the rest of the year. And interestingly enough, since I began winter angling March has been my most challenging month of the year, because often it produces the greatest amount of snowmelt.

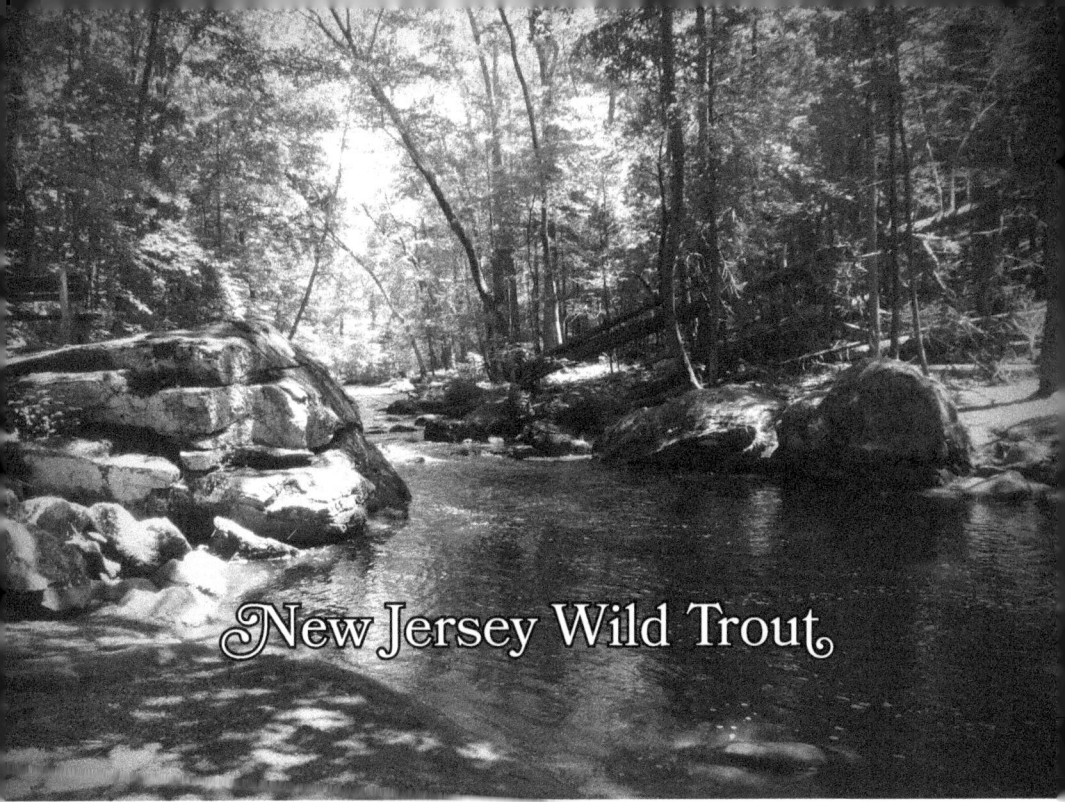

New Jersey Wild Trout

"**N**ew Jersey wild trout," now there's four words I never would have strung together consecutively in a phrase or sentence. And that includes the fact that I was born in Elizabeth, New Jersey, where I sprouted up through the early years of elementary school. Then our family relocated to Union, where I remained until graduating from Newark College of Engineering—now New Jersey Institute of Technology—afterward moving to upstate New York with my newly wedded bride.

In those Garden State years, I developed an acute passion for fishing when visiting my Uncle Pete at his Cranford home along the banks of the Rahway River. The river I wandered behind his house was filled with discarded tires, bedsprings, abandoned household appliances, decaying logs, chubs, and a few beautiful—in my eyes— hatchery trout. While I was staying with my uncle, he generously purchased a fishing rod for me, planting a seed within that still bears fruit sixty-plus years later.

In the beginning, although I pursued elusive Rahway River hatchery trout, I mostly caught sunfish and chubs, if I caught anything at all. Over time I would outgrow the Rahway, eventually exploring some of the Garden State's best-known trout waters, yet all with abundant hatchery fish: Big Flat Brook, Black River, the Raritan River's Ken Lockwood Gorge, and the Musconetcong, to name but a few. After my wife and I moved to New York, I soon learned about wild trout, cultivating a strong sense of appreciation for fish the Lord created and hatchery trucks didn't dump into a waterway. Enthusiastically, I became engaged in conservation endeavors while fishing as much as I could when not involved with family activities.

Fish I did, nine months out of every year from April 1st through the end of November, as the New York State trout season was eventually allowed on the Esopus Creek at the time. On November 30th, 2012, I whipped the creek to a froth while snowflakes filled the air and ice clogged the guides on my Orvis Battenkill. According to the canon law of the Church of Sir Izaak Walton, it was the last day of trout season, a piscatorial time of high obligation not to be missed. I never detected a hit that day, and that experience left a very sour taste in my mouth, ending the season in such fashion. After all, it was a long time until April 1st again.

Fortunately, early December 2012 Catskill weather was June-like, causing my piscatorial juices to flow like the sap of maple trees during warm spring days. Accordingly, I ventured over to the Willowemoc's no-kill section on December 5th to wet a line and drown a fly. I hadn't fished any December days since I was a teenager, when my longtime buddy Bill Nicol—aka Stickball Finn—and I flogged the Big Flat Brook, where a hatchery rainbow ate a salmon egg I drifted its way.

The Willow was my first Catskill love; thus, I was truly excited about that day trip. Fishing my Black Leech, I caught three brown trout up to fourteen inches in length and a foot-long smallmouth bass. I ended the outing having touched four fish: two wild ones and two of hatchery origin. That day triggered a new craving in me, producing a fresh bucket-list set of goals. At day's end, I vowed to pursue catching at least one trout every consecutive month of the year on a fly. Heck, I already had nine months accounted for through the end of 2012; I needed to catch only three more trout in early 2013. Really, how hard could that be?

In January 2013, my good buddy Tony Cocozza and I fished Connecticut's Farmington, where we froze, but I still managed to catch a small hatchery brown on a Black Leech. Then on Valentine's Day, I pounded New Jersey's Pequest River in the Trout Conservation Area near the hatchery outflow. At first I had this small piece of the water to myself, but then so many fly fishers arrived I had to be extra careful not to bang the tip of my cane rod on their rods while casting. This outing turned into one of the most unpleasant angling encounters I ever experienced. Clearly these anglers were putting "the Jersey squeeze" on me. Using a size 20 Dorato Hare's Ear, I missed a couple trout that rose, but eventually caught a fifteen-inch, badly worn hatchery rainbow that took a size 8 Black Conehead Woolly Bugger in a frothy flow. With that I departed the Pequest, and as I did two other fly fishers jumped into my spot. Really, is that what trout fishing is all about?

In early March, I planned to explore the West Branch of the Delaware River, which exhibited low flows while reporting decent winter hatches, but I came down with the flu and was bedridden for a bit. On March 11th, Tony Cocozza and I fished the Beaverkill and Willowemoc no-kills. Using my Black Leech, I nicked a foot-long brown on the Willow and almost had it to the net, but lost it, while my buddy Tony caught a sixteen-inch brown in each of these waters. That outing's outcome produced a profound difference in my trout fishing for many years to come, because March was not yet accounted for.

On March 18th, I wandered downstate to the Ramapo River on a very cold day, resulting in ice in my guides, while I never detected a single hit. With more than half the month now gone, I was beginning to lose hope of ever catching a March trout and not completing a twelve-month streak. That's when I received a phone call from my buddy Stickball Finn—we go back to elementary school days. Bill told me about a New Jersey wild-trout stream he fishes, though I never knew

New Jersey had any wild-trout streams. He told me we could meet there in pursuit of my March trout, but I couldn't reveal the stream's name or location. So I agreed.

Following GPS directions, on March 20th, I found Finn and his secret brook, which was clear and cold, with a nice winter flow. The creek was small water, which I like, yet with a slick, rocky bottom. I fished two favorite early season weighted nymphs, a size 12 Epeorus Nymph on point with a size 12 Muskrat dropper, on a short, tight line, high-sticking my way along. It took perhaps two dozen casts, with Bill watching the entire time, but soon I caught a small wild brown trout, and March was in the books. Thank you, Finn!

For a few hours, we fished a major portion of this hidden brook, flip-flopping around each other. Then warm weather caused snowmelt, with the brook turning an aqua color and trout stopped feeding. The snowmelt brought about a drop in the creek's pH and colder water temperatures, stressing fish. That outing ended with a half dozen six-to-ten-inch stunning wild browns and a new love for Garden State wild-trout waters. I would eventually return to this gem of a little hidden creek several times, even after major open-heart surgery.

In the years to come, New Jersey waters would provide my escape when it came to winter trout fishing. I scrutinized online maps, studied the *New Jersey Freshwater Fishing Digest*, cross-examined friends on the QT about these waters, and even purchased Matt Grobert's *Fly Fishing New Jersey Trout Streams*. I was hooked, and Jersey was reeling me in. Who could have believed this? Not me—that's for sure.

Perhaps my best source of information, other than what I gathered from a few good friends, was the *New Jersey Freshwater Fishing Digest* because it listed some thirty-plus streams that their Division of Fish and Wildlife classified as wild-trout waters. Jersey manages these waters differently than their stocked streams, and they are open to year-round angling, though part of the time only on a catch-and-release basis. However unlike New York, which often posts signage along waters open to public fishing, such is not always the case in the Garden State. The *Digest* provided general locations, but often, there was a lot of searching involved, and without firsthand knowledge an angler probably often wouldn't know where to fish.

Since my first New Jersey wild-trout outing in March of 2013, I have made an effort to fish at least half of the wild-trout waters listed in New Jersey's *Digest*, and eventually I've caught wild trout in all the waters I fished, though many times it required more than a single outing to accomplish that goal. Not to make excuses, but most of my fishing on those unknown waters was done from January through March, when bugs were nowhere to be found, and at times I trekked through knee-deep snow. Such conditions were not always the best for trout fishing, but often, it was just great to get outdoors when other anglers might be skiing, tying flies, or sitting by a fireplace somewhere. I've caught wild Garden State brook, brown, and rainbow trout from four inches long up to almost twenty-three inches in length. However, one of my fondest memories of wandering Garden State wild-trout waters did not occur during a chilly winter month, but rather on June 29th, 2018.

It was a Friday, and I volunteered to pick up our grandson Cooper after school, bringing him back home to spend the weekend with his New York State family. As I typically did on such trips, I combined the journey with fishing a Garden State stream. That day I chose to explore the Black River and its tributaries in Hacklebarney State Park. Despite what the title of Thomas Wolfe's 1940 posthumously published novel *You Can't Go Home Again* claimed, I wanted to relive a bit of my past.

Hacklebarney State Park is located between Long Valley and Chester in Morris County, consisting of roughly twelve hundred forested acres. The Black River cuts through the base of the park, cascading around boulders in the hemlock-lined ravine, while Rinehart Brook and Trout Brook tributaries add cool volume to its flow. Numerous waterfalls abound. Native Americans originally inhabited this glacial valley. In the early eighteenth century, agriculture was a way of life, with iron mines soon to follow, and for more than a century iron mines were worked where Hacklebarney is now located. The park was established in 1924 from land donated by Adolphe E. Borie (1866–1954), a Philadelphia lawyer, zinc-manufacturing merchant, and president of the Savage Arms Company, plus vice president of the Bethlehem Steel Corporation. Today, Hacklebarney is a favorite setting for avid hikers, nature lovers, picnickers, hunters, and anglers like me. Three rare and endangered plant species are found in its boundaries: American ginseng, leatherwood, and Virginia pennywort. Black bears, deer, foxes, and wild turkeys, plus numerous other wildlife species inhabit the park.

When I was growing up, my parents would often bring my twin sisters and me to Hacklebarney. My sisters played, and my parents sat on shaded lawn chairs reading, while I fished the Black River. The river was stocked with hatchery fish, but both tributaries support wild trout. I loved the Black River; in later years, when I could drive, I would fish it with worms, salmon eggs, and flies. The very first trout I ever caught on a fly I caught in Trout Brook on a White Irresistible dry. The image of that event is forever burned into the gray matter sitting above my shoulders, fresh as fresh can be. It was a little brook trout, and though I didn't know it at the time, it probably was the very first New Jersey wild trout I ever caught.

On this particular outing in 2018, I sought to relive my past, if nothing else, in memory of my parents. I hiked several park trails for old-time's sake and walked along the Black River where I had fished many times before. Back then I had even shared a date or two with my wife-to-be Lois during the start of our over half-century relationship. One of the first landscape paintings Lois ever did for me was of the Black River, when we had a picnic date day there. Years later, she tried to put that oil landscape into the garbage, but I secretly saved it. So yes, I really was trying to go home again.

On that June outing in 2018, I found Trout Brook to be skinny, chilly, and a tad stained from iron-rich sedimentary rocks. Along that tributary trek were numerous dog walkers, joggers, and kids tossing sticks and rocks into the well-shaded brook as it flowed through the base of a hollow. One kid even yelled out to me, "Hey mister, what fly are you fishing?"

Well, I was using a size 14 X-Caddis, my most trusted dry fly when results really matter. And I cast it with my 6½-foot Superfine cane rod, the first bamboo rod I ever owned. I rambled past the busy crowds and even moved a few fish along the way, but I wasn't sure any of these were trout. Then, under a splintered, worn wooden footbridge in a shaded run, a small wild brook trout ate my X-Caddis. I was home once again, catching a New Jersey wild trout where I probably did almost a half century before, without fully comprehending what I did at that moment.

I would catch one more brook trout before ending this adventure. Then, back at my Tacoma, I stowed my gear. I knew that I owe everything I have, everything I've become, to my parents, who worked so hard to make a better life for my sisters and me, and that these wild trout are only a small part of it.

Eighty-One

It was Monday evening, November 19th, 2018, and snow would soon be falling in the Catskill Mountains. Consequently, in the dark of the night our oldest daughter, my wife, and I secured a hotel room in Poughkeepsie, only two miles from Vassar Brothers Medical Center, because I had to be there at 5:30 the next morning. Thus, I was on time for seven-and-a-half hours of surgery, performed by two doctors who replaced my aortic valve and repaired an aneurysm. The surgery was a success, but I'd spend Thanksgiving and several more days at Vassar, recovering and conditioning myself to return home. My wife, Lois, became my constant and loving caregiver for the immediate future, while I was given a list of restrictions with limited physical activities allowed for at least six weeks to come. The last thing I wanted to do was disappoint my wife by not adhering to those carefully worded instructions provided upon my hospital release.

Nonetheless, back in 2012 I had started trying to catch at least one trout every consecutive month of the year on a fly. I had been doing such ever since, though with my heart surgery I expected this run would clearly end. However, on December 22nd, I finally was given permission to drive again. Just two weeks earlier, I had begun cardiovascular rehab and it was going better than expected. That old piscatorial flame still burned brightly within me. So I asked my wife if I could head to New Jersey and attempt to catch a December trout. I made promises I fully intended to keep, such as not wandering too far from my truck and not fishing more than an hour. I really didn't expect much, but I wanted to try anyway. To my surprise, Lois said "OK," but gave me strict orders to adhere to those self-imposed rules.

So with Christmas only three days away, with some trepidation, I drove I-87 south to New Jersey, slow and steady as she goes, wondering what I was doing the entire time. "Can I even do this?" "Am I still capable of wandering about outside on my own?" Thoughts of self-doubt filled my mind, yet onward I pressed. Late the previous night, I mentally walked through various angling scenarios: Where would be best place for me to fish, and what I should use? I had a plan and I had a backup plan, and I told my wife I would not deviate from either of these.

My first intended stop was at a national park where a tiny native brook trout creek slithers through its base. However, the federal government was in a partial shutdown mode, and this park was closed. Thus, I relocated to another nearby watershed containing wild brown trout, hidden in a suburban ravine in Morris County, one of the wealthiest small municipalities in the United States. That was not exactly where one might expect to fly fish for wild trout. However, it was part of the Green Acres Program, created in 1961 to meet the New Jersey's expanding recreation and conservation needs.

The parcel I intended to fish connected several contiguous natural areas, traversed by a pristine small wild brown trout stream. It offered hiking trails, a well-used escape for dog walkers, a noted waterfall, nature watching, colonial-era ruins, and of course fishing. Upon arrival, I encountered another fly fisher in the parking area, already getting ready to fish. I was shocked, because it was late December. Who actually fly fishes in December, with Christmas just three days away? Well, who else does, anyway?

I approached him, inquiring where he intended to fish and if I might fish the bridge pool next to the parking area, if he wasn't going to. He wasn't the friendliest of fellows, but he did tell me that I could have the bridge pool as he wandered away up into the hollow.

As I got ready, two of his buddies arrived, and we enjoyed a more pleasant conversation. I told them that their friend already had walked up the hill into a ravine across the road. I also told them about my recent heart surgery. Then I entered a clear, very cold brook that held a decent flow. I never fully tightened my waders, not wanting the straps to stress my shoulders and chest. And I stumbled about the stony slick bottom, trying to find my sea legs. At first this was a challenge, but luckily I had my wading staff because my stamina was less than I had hoped for. Slow and steady as she goes, that's how I moved about. And my casts were just short, quick tosses, not extending my right arm much at all. I high-sticked a short line with a size 12 Epeorus Nymph and size 14 Pink Squirrel dropper attached to my leader, the only part of my gear that cut through the water.

Slowly, I covered some twenty-five yards of creek, not expecting much, just happy to be standing upright the entire time and fishing. Eventually, I waded through the pool below the stone bridge, and soon, the foamy, turbulent inflow of a tiny backeddy was a rod length away. That's where Lady Luck smiled down upon me. I'd have only one hit, but sometimes one hit is all it takes. Soon enough, a nine-inch wild brown, that ate my Pink Squirrel, was flopping around on the stream's bank as I wore a big smile on my face. *Salmo trutta.* I wondered if this little wild brown trout was of English or German descent. It was small, but pretty, with dark brown spots along its back, red dots bounded by larger bluish halos along the lateral line, a soft, creamy-yellow belly, and perfectly formed translucent fins. My eighty-first consecutive month of catching a trout was in the books, and as I quit the two other fly fishers wandered over to inspect my trout before its release and congratulate me. Slowly and carefully, I drove back home.

Blood and Bamboo

It was only the second day of March 2020, but several years of winter fly fishing have taught me to strike while the iron was hot. The day's weather forecast called for blue skies with air temperatures pushing the mercury past the fifty-degree mark on outside thermometers. Thus, I found my way south on I-87, soon crossing over into the Garden State in pursuit of a March wild trout. There I snaked along country roads paralleling the state line, eventually passing Ringwood Manor, a National Historic Landmark and former home to Edward R. Hewitt, Abram S. Hewitt, Peter Cooper, and many of the Hewitt clan. Clearly, the countryside held an aristocratic tenor, yet there were many places that could have been mistaken for my beloved Catskills.

I parked on a dirt pullout on a semibusy road in a quiet rural neighborhood. The surrounding terrain was cloaked in brown garb, totally snowless, yet still supported winter's stillness. The hidden brook in the rocky ravine below was clear, with chilly flows well below the 50 percent seasonal trends according to a USGS gage located downstream.

Lacking snow, with perhaps a dry spring yet to occur, what might happen to these trout waters when summer finally arrives? But that was still distant in months ahead and not my main concern that morning. After all, I was there hoping to catch a March wild trout on a well-placed fly.

I ambled down into the ravine below, making my way around deadfalls that reached out trying to grab my feet, slowing me down, with boulders the size of picnic tables. Life at the base of this hollow was lacking, except for a few winter midges and the odd Little Black Stonefly. Pockets of ice still were present, and I measured the water temperature to be thirty-five degrees. I probed the brook with a size 8 Red Butt Conehead Woolly Bugger on point and a size 14 Pink Squirrel dropper—no sense changing what has been a working combination these last couple of winter months. Portions of the numerous mini plunge pools here often remained ice free in the secluded, stone-lined rift, even during the harshest winter weather.

Slowly, I negotiated the rocky terrain, half frozen and half thawed where dappled sunlight penetrated to its base. I paid more attention to where I fished than where I wandered, and that caused an issue. A rock the shape and size of a shoe box, rolled underfoot, made loose by thawed, soft earth, causing me to go down like the helpless Titanic. I have a lot of experience at falling while fishing, and typically, I gently toss my bamboo rod away from me, then brace my fall. However, on this outing I was totally surrounded by a miniature version of Stonehenge, and there was nowhere to toss the cane Battenkill safely. My choices were obvious and required a split-second response. Either fall on the rod, breaking the bamboo, or hold it above my head. I'd heal, the bamboo wouldn't, so, I raised the rod above my head as I went down. And down I went!

I thought for sure that I'd be fine, but my knees landed in the depression formed where the rock underfoot rolled. This caused me to plunge forward swiftly, crashing my face into solid granite. I banged my nose somewhat sternly, but luckily didn't break any teeth. It took a few minutes, but then I finally stood up, gathering my thoughts. Lacking a mirror and fishing alone, I couldn't fully assess my personal impairments, so I kept fishing—what else should I do? In short order, I caught my first trout, a small wild rainbow about eight inches long. Then as I released it, I noticed blood in the water,

Had I injured that trout? Why was it bleeding? No, it shot away like nothing happened at all. Then I quickly realized I was the one who was bleeding. So I took a pause, pinching my nose, eventually stopping the blood's flow. Fortunately for me, several months ago, my family doctor suggested that I stop taking Eliquis. Following open-heart surgery in late 2018, I had a minor atrial fibrillation incident and was put on Eliquis for several months. Subsequent tests indicated I was fine, and over the objection of my cardiologist, my primary care doctor knowing my lifestyle recommended I stop taking that high-priced blood thinner. At my wife's request, I had visited the family doctor after a different fall while fishing. The lower right side of my body had turned purple from that fall and my primary care physician's exact words were, "If you ever did this to your head, we wouldn't be talking today!"

Those memories obscured my mind as I went back to fishing that March morning. However, I only fished for one hour that day, covering some two hundred and fifty yards of a gorgeous brook in a rocky hollow. During that time, I caught five small wild Garden State rainbows up to nine inches long, all colorful crimson gems, some dark as mortal sin. I didn't want to push my luck, because I promised my wife that I'd be careful. When I arrived home much earlier than planned, she asked me, "So, what did you do—did you fall again?"

Well yes, I did. But, my bamboo rod was in one piece and my ninety-sixth consecutive month of catching at least one trout on a fly was successfully, though painfully, accounted for.

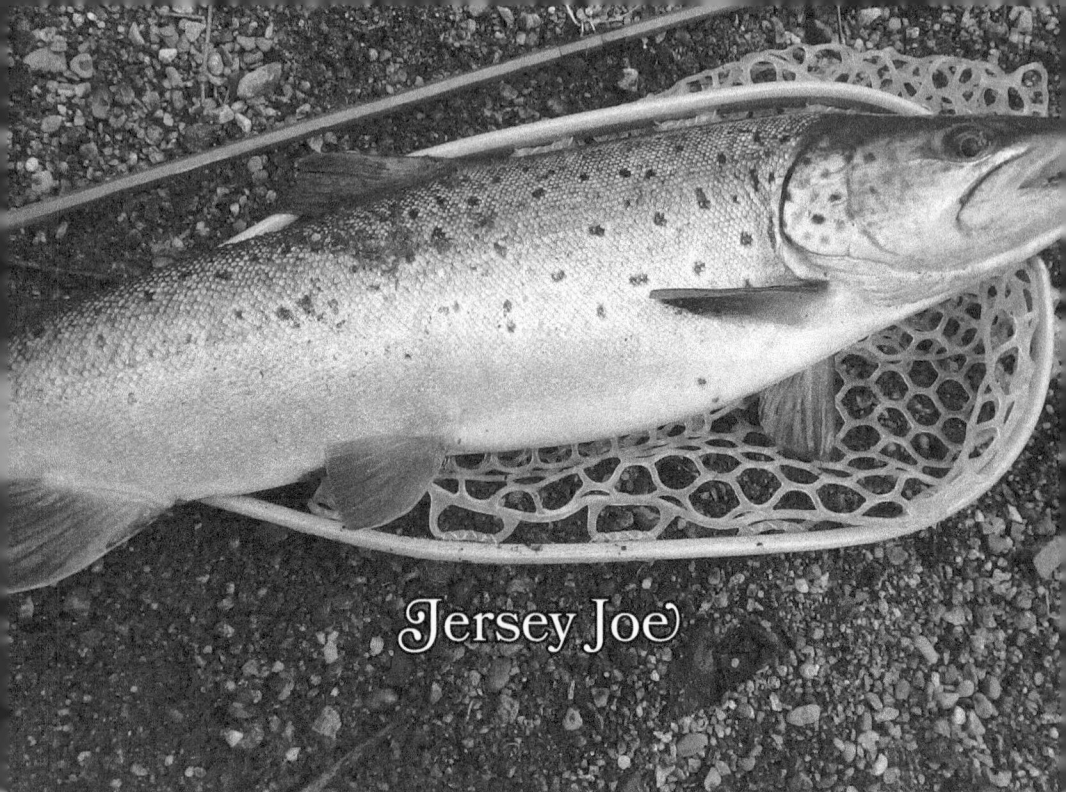

Jersey Joe

On April 8th, 2016 I tangled with Jersey Joe, and stunned by the outcome of the battle with this heavyweight.

Dating back to April of 2012, I'd been on a crazy crusade trying to catch at least one trout each consecutive month of every year on a fly, and since March of 2013 I sought to only count wild trout caught on a fly, size not a factor at all. Knowing I could not fully accomplish this task in my home state of New York, I pursued out-of-state nonresident fishing licenses. The first January of 2013, after attempting this goal, found me driving due east to explore Connecticut's Farmington River with my good buddy Tony Cocozza.

I was excited about that outing and had a hard time sleeping the night before. Air temperatures that day were forecast to be in the mid-forties and we hoped to find trout rising to tiny winter caddis. However, on our drive over outside temperatures never exceeded the twenty-three-degree mark, while shrubs and trees along the way were coated with a thin film of fresh, translucent ice.

The Farmington looked picture perfect though, and eventually air temperatures broke the freezing point. However, it remained very cold and the fishing was hard at best. Ice continually clogged our fly-rod guides. We tried our luck in Whittemore and Church Pools, ending these long, chilly efforts with just three hits on my part. However, that last hit resulted in one ten-inch hatchery brown in a run below the Route 318 bridge. That fish took a size 10 Black Leech fished slow and deep as the sun disappeared for the day. Dumb luck at best, but at least I had a trout in the tenth consecutive month of my self-proclaimed crusade.

March 2013 would be a struggle, too. I came down with the flu, spending part of the month in bed. Then I tried fishing the Beaverkill and Willowemoc no-kill sections before heading south to explore the Ramapo River. I struck out in all these places, never catching a fish. With about a week left in the month and no trout touched, my long-time buddy Bill Nicol suggested we fish a New Jersey wild-trout stream. Heck, I grew up in New Jersey and never knew the Garden State had any wild-trout streams.

So together we wandered a little brook tucked away in a suburban hollow. As luck would have it, we both caught a half dozen small, gorgeous wild browns on Schwiebert's Epeorus Nymph before warm weather and snowmelt shut the creek down. That outing opened my eyes to look south if I wanted to catch trout during winter months, where seasonal weather should be a tad warmer. I soon studied the *New Jersey Freshwater Fishing Digest* for other Garden State wild-trout waters to wander during the cold months of December through March, finding a list of several options to explore.

During the winter months, with snow and ice about, with cold water—sometimes only slightly above the freezing point—and with few bugs active, it can be difficult to reconnoiter new trout waters never wandered before, but I've always found it exiting to get out of the house, meandering nature on the warmest days winter has to offer. Systematically, I attacked Jersey's list of wild-trout streams. Sometimes

I'd get lucky and catch a wild trout on the first visit, but many times, it required more than a single trip to succeed. One such river was the Wanaque.

The Wanaque's source is Greenwood Lake, which straddles the New York–New Jersey state line in the shadows of the Ramapo River Valley and is a major tributary of the Pequannock River. The Wanaque was once known as Long Pond River, because Greenwood Lake was once called Long Pond. Downstream of Wanaque Reservoir, the lower river is a short tailwater in the general vicinity of I-287. It's not a typical tailwater, like those found in the Catskills, though it does remind me a little of the lower Neversink, yet it doesn't seem to be nearly as cold. Plus, there is a sewage treatment outlet below the Raymond Dam that offends one's nose, not to mention that the mucky river bottom releases hydrogen sulfide bubbles that smell, plus holding debris that can tangle flies. Still, it was on my list of Jersey wild-trout streams to fish.

It would take several trips over the course of a couple years before I finally caught a Wanaque wild trout. However, I did hook and lose a nice brown on the first visit, but then there was a very long silent spell. Reports suggested the Wanaque held some nice browns, but hardly any small wild trout. The river also supports bass and pickerel. Perhaps those warmwater fish feast on little wild trout, that appear to be missing. In any event, on April 8th, 2016, I finally caught my first few browns and what a memorable day it was.

That day, my wife and I made a trip to Jersey to pick up a grandson after school. Since we had some free time and it was only a short detour from our intended journey, I stopped to fish the Wanaque while my wife read a book. I fished my Black Leech and was soon rewarded with a twelve-inch brown, followed by another that measured thirteen and a half inches. Then I moved downstream, crossing the river via the Indian Rock Trail. There, in the brush-lined narrow run below, I experienced a crushing strike from a Lord's Prayer trout.

A really nice fish thrashed the water, jumping once, rolling about the stream's surface. It took a while and several times I had to reposition myself downstream of the brute, forcing it to fight the river's current as well as me. As the brown tired, almost to the net, it wrapped itself about a partially submerged branch. Well, Lady Luck smiled upon me and my unsteady hands freed the trout from this tangle. Eventually I beached a 22½-inch brown, which I measured three times just to be sure of the exact length. At that time, that trout was one of the largest browns I ever caught outside of a Great Lakes tributary stream, exceeded in length only by Iron Mike—a twenty-three-inch Neversink brown that also succumbed to a Black Leech.

After taking a couple of quick photographs of the big brown, I released it and quit for the day. Then once back at my truck, I showed my wife photos of the trout, which she dubbed Jersey Joe.

Netflix

Growing up, I seemed to have a natural aptitude for math, like my dad, but I loved history—especially American history. Thus, when it came time to make a college decision, I gave thought to pursuing a degree in history, but my father asked me, "How are you going to make a living with that?" So I pursued an engineering degree, something my dad always wanted to do, only World War II and we kids got in his path. However, as an engineer, I chose an easy route, that of an industrial engineer, but it did make good use of my mathematical skills.

Fast-forward to the twenty-first century. A few months ago, my wife suggested that we subscribe to Netflix, as most of her friends had already done. It's always been my goal to make her happy, even if it meant "keeping up with the Joneses". Hence, we subscribed, and I'm glad we did. Every day when exercising on the treadmill, I'd watch a Netflix show for about an hour, and just like that, four miles were easily done. In fact, most days, I'd log over five miles and had Netflix to thank for that.

One of my favorite series was a chronicle about the American Revolution titled *Turn*. It was a story based upon an actual 1770s family, featuring a Long Island cabbage farmer named Abraham Woodhull. Woodhull was born in Setauket in 1750 and became a main member of the Culper Spy Ring, which provided intelligence to George Washington for the Patriots' war efforts. In support of his labors, Woodhull used the alias Samuel Culper as he traveled the local countryside. Many of the scenes depicted nearby settings throughout New York, New Jersey, and Pennsylvania. While watching *Turn*, I looked forward to exercising every day and yearned to return to Jockey Hollow, where George Washington's army camped during the winter of 1779–80.

The last time I did so was just seven days prior to my heart surgery. I fished Jockey Hollow National Park and caught a small wild brook trout on a size 16 Adams, putting November 2018 in the books, much to my pleasant surprise. However, as of February 2020 I hadn't wandered the hollow since then, until February 12th of that year.

That morning brought air temperatures comfortably in the high thirties under a bluish-pewter sky. The surrounding national park terrain sported a drab brown, winter worn-out look, while Father Time and climate change seem to be taking their toll on the diminutive brook that cuts through the base of this historic hollow. It used to be that on a good day, a well-placed fly might interest two dozen little wild brook trout. Nowadays, a half dozen tiny fish touched seemed to be a very good number.

Following a late start, I trekked about a mile down over a half-frozen and half-slick muddy trail into a recess steeped in antiquity. Along the way, I stepped around fresh piles of horse manure left behind by mounted riders. Soon I came upon a decent seasonal flow of a clear, cold tiny brook bounded by the wet terrain. All about, eastern skunk cabbage poked up through the muck. Otherwise, the hollow was almost lifeless, except for the rare midge fly taking flight.

Initially, I fished with my favorite winter dry fly, a size 18 Dorato Hare's Ear. Dropping the dry in likely looking places, I never brought a single fish to the surface. Thus, I added a size 20 Copper John dropper nymph some six inches below the dry fly. Still not much happened.

Eventually, though, the Dorato was attacked with all the furor and might that a seven-inch wild brook trout could muster. After that, it was a measured, slow go again, but as the noon hour approached, activity improved. I nicked several fish that held beneath an undercut bank, catching two more steak-fry-sized brookies on the Copper John. I also spooked a decent trout and watched a few rising fish ignore my offerings before the Dorato Hare's Ear accounted for three final brook trout by the time I quit.

I wandered a historic hollow for two hours one February morning catching six Garden State wild brook trout, mostly steak-fry size, but one a solid seven inches. These fish probably were descendants of trout that navigated this brook when Washington's Continental Army wintered here, and that made them special in my eyes. Thankfully, Jersey freshwater fishing regulations have special provisions for these wild brook trout, progenies of our revolution.

This outing reminded me of a quote attributed Henry David Thoreau, "Many men go fishing all their lives without knowing it is not fish they are after," but more likely paraphrased from a January 26th, 1853 Thoreau Journal entry.[1]

---

[1] Jeffrey S. Cramer, curator, Walden Woods Project's Thoreau Institute, personal communication, February 18, 2022.

Olives

Blue-Winged Olives are an underappreciated Esopus Creek hatch when compared with the celebrated reputation of *Isonychia*; yet I love them. Even though hatches are sometimes sparse and of short duration, they recur all season long. I willingly admitted in *Ramblings of a Charmed Circle Flyfisher* that I'm not a bug expert by any stretch of one's imagination. In fact, my mode of operation when it comes to trout flies is to use generic patterns that confused and bewildered trout might take for any one of several of favorite meals. Classic dry flies representing celebrated hatches such as Hendricksons, March Browns, Light Cahills, or whatever have never been in my piscatorial repertoire. Still, I have pondered aquatic bugs since first reading Art Flick's *Streamside Guide* and Ernest Schwiebert's *Matching the Hatch* as a teenage wannabe fly fisher more than half a century ago. It's just none of that entomology stuff sunk in and took hold. But at least I tried.

Blue-Winged Olives made their impression upon me in the early

1970s after I acquired a copy of J. W. Dunne's *Sunshine and the Dry Fly*. Dunne devoted an entire chapter to this subject and started by asking the question, "What is a blue upright?"[1] Well, if this noted English author, distinguished British military officer, aeronautical engineer, and philosopher didn't know, then how could a young wannabe trout fisher like me ever know? To be totally honest, I call most small dark mayflies I encounter Olives and fish Olive imitations accordingly.

Celebrated angling author John Gierach included various stories about Olives in several of his books. In *Another Lousy Day in Paradise*, Gierach lamented, "some things in life seem unfair" … "the best Blue-winged Olive Mayfly hatch of the year" comes during Colorado deer season, when he is hunting.[2] Then, in *No Shortage of Good Days*, Gierach finds himself on an elk hunt "when the Blue-winged Olive hatch can be on."[3] In the Catskills, there are frequently wonderful Olive hatches on cold, snowy, winterlike days, and they can be exciting. When these occur, it's often only a matter of time before most surface-feeding trout activity will be done for the season, so one had better slow down and enjoy the moment. Blue-Winged Olive hatches tend to be foul-weather insects, hatching when the less hardy fly fishers stay home, leaving me more places to cast my dry flies over rising trout. In *A Fly Rod of Your Own*, Gierach embraces "trying to pick out the gray, rainy days that both the trout and mayflies like" for fishing Blue-Winged Olives.[4]

As Ed Engle wrote in a *Fly Tyer* article, "Blue-winged Olives are a diverse, widespread group, and probably the most common small mayflies. Imitating them entails tying a variety of patterns."[5] Over the years, I've tried many different Olive patterns, from Parachutes, to Comparaduns, to Usual variations, to hackled dries, plus a fair number of CDC concoctions, with my current favorites noted below. They

[1] J. W. Dunne, *Sunshine and the Dry Fly* (London: Adam and Charles Black, 1950), p. 67.
[2] John Gierach, *Another Lousy Day in Paradise* (New York: Simon & Schuster, 1966), p. 116.
[3] John Gierach, *No Shortage of Good Days* (New York: Simon & Schuster, 2011), p. 183.
[4] John Gierach, *A Fly Rod of Your Own* (New York: Simon & Schuster, 2017), p. 138.
[5] Ed Engle, "Olives," *Fly Tyer*, Autumn–Winter 1996, pp. 12–16 and 78.

vary in size and color throughout the season also. As Engel also wrote: "early *Baetis* hatches tend to consist of larger (size 18 and 20) mayflies that are lighter in color. Autumn *Baetis* hatches are significantly darker and smaller. These mahogany-and-olive duns range from size 20 down to 26."[6] While Engel was referring to Western rivers, I found these comments to be valid on waters I fish.

Depending on the season and where I'm fishing, I carry several small boxes of different Olive patterns in varying sizes, many of which stay in my truck until needed. In recent years during the spring, my preferred dry is a size 16 Olive Comparadun. In *Tying Small Flies*, where Engel dedicates an entire chapter to Olives, he notes how effective it is to fish "a dropper twelve to eighteen inches behind a *Baetis* dry fly,"[7] So, sometimes I add a size 16 or size 18 Pheasant Tail Nymph some six inches below my dry fly. As trout season wears on and summer pushes into autumn, I turn to a size 18 or 20 Dorato Hare's Ear, and if these don't work, I drop down to a size 22 or 24 Mahogany Slant-Wing CDC, a creation of my own.

All of this these choices were motivated by Engel's article. To read about them in action, join me on a few seasonal outings where Blue-Winged Olives ruled.

May 10th, 2016. The Esopus looked fine; the Portal was closed, and river flows were dropping and clearing following heavy rains. During the morning, I worked outside the house, but then cloudy skies followed me to the legendary Chimney Hole. There, the Esopus was on fire with rising trout all about. Initially, I fished a size 14 X-Caddis, but quickly changed over to a size 16 Blue-Winged Olive Comparadun, and that made all the difference. Before quitting, I released over three dozen iridescent rainbows. Most of these were cookie-cutter size nine-to-eleven-inch fish with small heads, yet lion hearts, silver-sided warriors, each with an in-your-face attitude. One of the 'bows cleared water by a good

---

[6] Ibid.
[7] Ed Engle, *Tying Small Flies* (Mechanicsburg, PA: Stackpole Books, 2004), p. 86.

three feet. This was the Esopus that Ray Ovington wrote about when he said, "the Esopus has been good to all of us, especially me."[8]

May 2nd, 2019. The Esopus was absolutely gin clear and at a perfect flow. The New York City Department of Environmental Protection had retained contractors to work on Schoharie Reservoir's infrastructure, including the Shandaken Tunnel. Thus, there were no Portal diversions to the Esopus Creek. That afternoon was cloudy, chilly, and raw, with Blue-Winged Olives on the water again. It was the third consecutive day I fished my Esopus, this time in a favorite pool. I never wandered more than twenty yards and for the most part used only a size 16 Blue-Winged Olive Comparadun. By the time I quit, I had caught almost two dozen 'bows and one small wild brown. Most of the rainbows were ten to eleven inches long, with a few shorter, and a half dozen twelve-to-fourteen-inches. Most of these were chrome sided, with many leapers among them. All of them were strong fighters. Once again, Ovington's words above rang true.

June 18th, 2019. Joe David, John Julian, and Bill Nicol—the Jersey Boys—came north to search for *Isonychia* mayflies along the Esopus Creek, but the hatch was not very cooperative. Joe and I fished Hudler's Flat, where we encountered a few sporadic risers. However, catching any of those using my Iso imitations was tough. As Joe wandered past me, he mentioned he caught a few rainbows on a Blue-Winged Olive dry fly, so I attached a size 16 Blue-Winged Olive Comparadun, which once again made the difference. I ended my evening with sixteen trout, thirteen of them rainbows, including five fish twelve to thirteen inches long. Most of those took the Blue-Winged Olive Comparadun.

October 29th, 2019. Rain had been falling for days, with Shandaken Tunnel still closed due to ongoing intake renovation. The Esopus flowed heavy, but not as much upstream of Phoenicia, since many of its major tributaries enter the main stream downstream of that hamlet. I planted myself in Excelsior Pool, where the river was elevated, but clear. Initially, I worked the pool hard with a streamer with a weighted

---

[8] Ray Ovington, *The Trout and the Fly* (New York: Hawthorn Books, 1977), p. 156.

nymph dropper attached above it. While this produced several hits, it didn't account for a single fish. Then I noticed a few trout rising in the pool's lower end.

That was another chilly, cloudy, and windy day, with a chop on the Esopus—not the best conditions for dry-fly fishing, especially with small flies. However, tiny Olives drifted past me, so I extended my leader with 6X tippet and attached a size 20 Dorato Hare's Ear. I stood shivering in cold water, waiting for the wind to stop so I could cast to rising targets. In a couple of hours' time, I caught nine small wild trout on the tiny Dorato Hare's Ear: five browns up to eleven inches long and four small rainbows, all with attitude and personality. By the time I wandered off this pool, my feet were like clay bricks, heavy and nonresponsive from the cold water.

November 13th, 2014. Both air and water temperatures sat in the low forties when I started fishing under an overcast raw sky. It was borderline nasty, but it would only get worse, with snow forecast for later in the day. The Esopus was clear, with a decent height and flow, but cold. At first, I fished a favorite pool with my Black Leech, slow and deep, catching four big browns from sixteen-plus to twenty inches. These results should have made me happy and quit, but I noticed Blue-Winged Olives starting to pop off the river, so I relocated, below the Five Arches Bridge, seeking a different experience.

I came upon a pool with trout boiling on the surface, rising every-where. Accordingly, I extended my leader adding 6X tippet and a size 18 Dorato Hare's Ear. This accounted for three trout, but I missed far more than I caught. Thus, I switched over to a size 22 Mahogany Slant-Wing CDC, and that made all the difference. By the time I quit, my dry flies picked up another dozen and a half wild trout up to eleven inches in length: eleven browns and seven rainbows. I enjoyed the best the Esopus had to offer: some big browns on a streamer early, then pin-point casting to selective, surface-feeding trout. With the end of trout season about two weeks away, that experience would stay with me through winter yet to come.

December 5th, 2013. The outing's high temperature peaked in the upper thirties, plus, it was breezy and cloudy, perhaps not the best day to fish dry flies. Nonetheless, I fished the Hazel Bridge Pool on the Willowemoc, because trout season was still open in this no-kill section. Initially, I fished a Conehead Woolly Bugger slow and deep, which resulted in a ten-inch smallmouth bass, but no trout. Then I noticed dimples here and there. Minuscule Olives were on the water. Thus, I lengthened my leader using 7X tippet and attached a size 24 Mahogany Slant-Wing CDC. Since I had expected to be tossing a streamer, I was using an 8-foot 6-weight Battenkill, not the best choice for 7X tippet. So when the trout started rising to my offerings, I didn't use the best hook-setting technique. In fact, I broke off the first three trout that rose by striking too hard and fast. Eventually I settled down, just tightening the line, gently raising the cane rod, and not striking at all. Using that improved technique, I landed three brown trout up to fourteen inches long before quitting.

Blue-Winged Olives—one has to love them. They defy adverse weather and just keep doing their thing. What I really like about the spring Esopus Creek Olive hatches is that they provide the opportunity to catch some nice rainbows that recently spawned, yet are still in the river before dropping back downstream to the Ashokan Reservoir. While late in the season, these hatches offer the last chance to catch a trout on a dry fly before winter takes control of these mountains. As Ted Leeson noted in *The Habits of Rivers*, "Where the great number of aquatic insects that interest fly fishermen undergo but one emergence a year, the Blue-Winged Olives just keep laying eggs and growing nymphs and hatching flies and feeding trout, heedless of calendars, even in winter." [9]

One has to love Olives, nasty weather and all.

---

[9] Ted Leeson, *The Habits of Rivers: Reflections on Trout Streams and Fly Fishing* (New York: Lyons Press, 1994), p. 39.

Sunday School

But there the Lord will be with us in majesty,

a place of broad rivers and streams.

—A version of Isaiah 33:21.

In our family's younger developing years, my wife taught Sunday school to youthful elementary-school-age kids, while I worked with middle and high-school-age students mainly because I've related well with this age group, eventually becoming a middle school teacher myself. We were fairly active in that church, forming many long-lasting friendships with other families and their children. So it was only natural that when a couple of former Sunday school students wanted to fish, I'd was only too happy to oblige.

May 11th, 2019. I assisted Trout Unlimited chapter members plant trees and shrubs along the East Branch Delaware River in Halcottsville. The weather was great and we enjoyed a good turnout. Then at 2:00 PM, I met Michael Barrette in Boiceville to fish the Esopus Creek with him. I've known Mike and the Barrette family for decades. They are as unrivaled as they come and were longtime members of the church before relocating south. Mike had recently moved from Virginia to Washington, DC, but was still an avid New York Mets fans and a career employee of the Environmental Protection Agency. Throughout the afternoon, we shared many interesting discussions about the status of the environment. He also told me that he had my wife as a Sunday school teacher, but never me, though I did teach his younger twin brothers. Mike had come north to visit some friends, open his Adirondack camp, and fish a bit. So he contacted me and I was glad he did.

The Esopus looked great—clear and at a perfect flow—but was bugless under a bright blue sky. The river was quiet and trout were nowhere to be found when we started. We were hoping to find some spring *Isonychia* nymphal shucks lining the rocks, but the spring hatch ran late that year. Initially we wandered Chimney Hole, where I thought afternoon shade might turn the fish on. A few trout did rise very sporadically here and there, but for the most part, it was RIP dead. The high point at this legendary hole was a bald eagle we kicked out upon arriving. Before moving upstream to the Trestle, I managed to fool one small rainbow on a size 16 Blue-Winged Olive Comparadun, but that was it.

The Trestle Pool was dead also, lying under bright sunlight, yet we did observe a couple of one-time risers to who knows what. We relocated one last time, upstream to Big Bend Pool, which was occupied by two spin fishers on the opposite bank. Fishing was slow, at best, but after the spinning duo left, trout rose sporadically where they once stood. I put Mike at the head of the pool, where a few trout rose, and fished blind downstream of him. Casting to trout that rose in the blink of an eye, we tried dropping our dry flies across fast water into a narrow, slower current seam along the river's edge. We each nicked a few trout using Blue-Winged Olive Comparaduns before I finally hooked a fourteen-inch tail-walking 'bow. It put up an impressive tussle and soon was flopping about on the rocky shoreline. After its quick release, we cast our flies a bit longer, but Mike had dinner plans with a high school buddy, so we called it a day, and a fine day it was, with a good friend on a beautiful stream.

And then there was Kemp Anderson. We've known the Andersons as long as we've known the Barrettes. In fact, I'm Kemp's younger brother David's godfather. We had these young men in Sunday school also, plus, Kemp did a fantastic job remodeling our family room.

Kemp and I had been talking about fishing the upper reaches of Warner Creek for some time. Back in 2015 and 2017, Tony Cocozza and I fished this remote region of the Phoenicia Wild Forest and Indian Head Wilderness, which drains Plateau Mountain with water so pristine one might drink it on the spot. Tony was going to join us, but then plans prevented that from happening.

June 2, 2018. It was a perfect day to wander into the middle of nowhere, experiencing the Catskills as they might have been in the late 1800s and early 1900s. Plus, the Esopus was roaring, with flows from the first 2018 recreational water release weekend. When Tony and I first attempted this adventure years ago, we tied bright yellow ribbons to trees so we could find our way in and out again. Those ribbons helped guide us into the wild glen below, a place where silence is broken by the sounds of nature alone.

That afternoon, after Kemp and I reached the belly of the forested ravine, we crossed a superb-looking Warner Creek and then trekked downstream on an old woods path leading away from Plateau Mountain. The setting was vintage Catskills: numerous small waterfalls and plunge pools, with rhododendrons and hemlocks all about. I told Kemp to expect to catch native brook trout, but not to be surprised to touch a few wild brown trout and rainbows mixed in among them. Seeing some small stoneflies airborne over the water, I suggested Kemp use a size 14 Elk Hair Stonefly dry fly, while I fished two small weighted nymphs, just to be different.

The young, energetic dry-fly fisher and I flipped around each other for a few hours, lost in the moment and wilderness setting. Making short, pinpoint casts while wandering through the dense forest, we negotiated Volkswagen-sized boulders, clear, cold mini pools, and greasy cobble underfoot, but rarely noticed a trout rise. Yet our efforts were rewarded with flashy, quick rises and aggressive strikes from headwater fish where life is a challenge in the long shadows of Little Rocky. By the time we quit, collectively, we caught over one hundred wild trout, mostly five-to-nine-inch native brookies, but with a handful of vibrant browns and 'bows, also.

The scenery was wild and rugged, and the company was great. Environs like this have long been my outdoor church, where artful Sunday school lessons can be taught. To share this with a former student was extraspecial. To quote Norman Maclean, the son of a Presbyterian minister and author of *A River Runs Through It*, "My father was very sure about certain matters pertaining to the universe. To him, all good things—trout as well as eternal salvation—come by grace and grace comes by art and art does not come easy."[1]

---

[1] Norman Maclean, *A River Runs Through It* (Chicago: University of Chicago Press, 1976), p. 4.

Silver Bullets[1]

DHE Basic

ost serious fly fishers seek a "silver bullet," a dry fly that will seduce finnicky trout when every other pattern in overcrowded fly boxes has failed miserably. For me, it's long been a Dorato Hares Ear. A few years ago, a fly-fishing buddy and Catskill Fly Tyers Guild member, Dave Plummer, put me on to this dry fly.

William C. Dorato (1915–2000), known as Willie to his good friends, and a native of Albany, New York, was an avid, accomplished fly fisher and fly tyer. He was also a founding member and first president of the Clearwater Chapter of Trout Unlimited who fished with the likes of Dud Soper, Dick Talleur, Art Flick, Frank Mele, Tony Bonavist, Del Bedinotti, and many other celebrated anglers. He frequented the Catskills, especially the Delaware system, plus the Battenkill near his home grounds. And it was on the Battenkill that he conceived the Dorato Hare's Ear while trying to imitate the hopping caddis that were

---

[1] A version of this chapter appeared in the January 2018 *Gazette*, newsletter of the Catskill Fly Tyers Guild.

prevalent on the river. According to longtime friend Del Bedinotti, Dorato's fly "created the illusion of movement due to the mix of wood duck wings and brown and grizzly hackle" its body of hare's mask, "complete with spikes," acting like additional hackle legs.[2]

The late Dick Talleur thought enough of Dorato and his dry fly that he gave special mention to both in at least two of his many angling books. In *Mastering the Art of Fly-Tying*, Talleur called Bill a "highly skilled and astute" tyer who can tie "classic patterns with the best," yet "his fly-box contains a vast array of nondescript, subtly seductive creations."[3] In *Trout Flies for the 21st Century* Talleur included three different variations of the Dorato Hare's Ear (DHE) recommending that it is best tied in sizes 10 to 16. Included were the basic DHE originated by Dorato, plus a Light and Gray Dun DHE, the work of Talleur's creativity and love of the pattern.

Talleur's feelings about the fly were expressed in an email he sent me several years ago. He wrote, "The DHE is still one of my main go-to flies. A few years ago, on the Farmington in CT, I hooked a huge brown on a size 14 Light Dorato, just at dusk. I played it for quite a while, finally it wrapped me around a rock, and that was the ball game. I'm pretty sure it would have been the biggest trout I ever caught."[4]

Both Eric Leiser, in *The Book of Fly Patterns*, and Terry Hellekson, in *Fish Flies*, include a little information on this dry fly, but other than that the average fly tyer might be hard-pressed to locate much material on the fly. I felt very lucky that Dave Plummer introduced me to the pattern several years ago, and it is now one of my main go-to dry flies for finicky, large, surface-feeding brown trout on tailwaters such as the West and East Branches of the Delaware, plus the Neversink below New York City's dam. It's also produced hard-to-move trout on Catskill freestone streams such as the Esopus and Willowemoc, and just a few summers past, it accounted for its share of cutthroat trout in

[2] Del Bedinotti, personal communication, March 5, 2010.
[3] Richard W. Talleur, *Mastering the Art of Fly-Tying* (Harrisburg, PA: Stackpole Books, 1979), p. 203.
[4] Richard W. Talleur, personal communication, n.d.

Yellowstone. I like to fish a Dorato Hare's Ear when caddis are about and also in small sizes when late-season Blue-Winged Olives are active. I tie the pattern in sizes 16 to 20, but a size 18 is by far my preferred choice under almost all conditions.

Del Bedinotti and Dick Talleur were in agreement on the pattern for a basic Dorato Hare's Ear:

> Thread: Camel or brown
> Wing: Wood duck
> Tail: Brown and grizzly hackle barbs, tied very short
> Body: Hare's ear mask with spikey guard hairs
> Hackle: Brown and grizzly mixed

I can recall many a fine Catskill outing when nothing else has worked, but a tiny Dorato Hare's Ear saved my bacon. There have been numerous late autumn outing on my Esopus when a size 18 or 20 DHE seduced wild rainbows and browns that were sipping miniscule Blue-Winged Olives. The same has been true on the no-kill sections of the Willowemoc and Beaverkill, and I've forgotten how many times large browns on the East Branch of the Delaware and its twin sister, the West Branch, have been fooled by my tiny DHEs. During the height of the COVID-19 pandemic, in mid-October of 2020, I enjoyed a very successful late-day outing with them on the Neversink below New York City's reservoir.

That day, the Neversink was low, clear, and chilly under a sky of increasingly thickening pewter-colored clouds. Its flow was glasslike, skinny and fragile; limited wading would be involved. Slowly and carefully, I inched my way along the stone-and-sand bottom. Several small tan caddis and tiny Blue-Winged Olives were about, and small trout punched holes in the stream's surface. At first, I fished a size 20 Mahogany Slant-Wing CDC dry fly. Zip. Then I switched to a size 18 Once and Away Emerger, a go-to fly pattern under such tough conditions. It quickly seduced a fat 16-inch brown, but then lost its magic.

With both caddis and Blue-Winged Olives about, I resorted to with my silver bullet, a size 20 Dorato Hare's Ear.

After waiting and watching for a target to cast at, I hooked and netted a twenty-one-inch brown, followed by a fifteen-inch brown, then lost my last nice fish of this outing, all of these while sight fishing to rising targets with a tiny DHE attached to 6X tippet. Then, during the last thirty minutes, the bugs disappeared, crowds arrived, the Neversink died, and I never observed another rising fish, so I quit.

I want to thank Dave Plummer, who uses two grizzly hackle tips instead of brown and grizzly hackle barbs for the tails on his Doratos, for introducing me to this dry fly. Several other variations of this pattern exist, as is the case for most successful trout flies, Plus, I would be remiss if I didn't thank Tony Bonavist and Del Bedinotti for background information used to pull this chapter together.

Mr. Spundun

We fellow beings wander this sphere known as the earth hoping to build strong and lasting bonds, valued friendships with like-minded people. In my case, Mr. Spundun fit that bill.

As a young wannabe angler, I read the major outdoor magazines: *Field & Stream*, *Outdoor Life*, and *Sports Afield*. I couldn't get enough of these periodicals, wearing ink right off the pages while perusing them. Then, later in life, as specialized fly-fishing publications exploded on the scene, I selectively embraced a few of those replacing the old standard magazines. Nowadays, in an age of pervasive electronic technology and reliance on the internet, it seems few folks support monthly subscriptions and newsprint publications any longer. However, I still value and hoard many of those older magazines that I read along my journey, now tucked away on book shelves, gathering dust. Sometimes they come in handy in unexpected ways.

That's how my good buddy Tony Cocozza—Mr. Spundun—got his name. Tony is a slender, wiry guy with a spring in his step, a broad smile on his face, and a personality to match, plus a can-do attitude and strong sense of community service. His high school yearbook noted that he was "not a sinner, not a saint perhaps, but well the best of chaps," with a great personality. As a 1962 West Orange Cowboys high school graduate who aspired to be an accountant, he wore number eleven on his back and won a scholarship, eventually played basketball for Upsala College. Their college motto was *Vincit omnia veritas*—truth conquers all. Never an accountant, he went on to be a public-school teacher, as I eventually would also. And he's quite the accomplished fly fisher for trout, but winter fishing is not his thing. He can get cold standing next to a roaring woodstove that time of year.

Both Tony and I have been active in the same Trout Unlimited chapter for decades, and we've participated in more than a few fishing excursions together. We've long worked shoulder to shoulder on several TU committees while jointly attending numerous public meetings in support of local Catskill rivers. It was Tony who introduced me to the Farmington River on one very cold January outing. And it was with Tony that I sought my first Saw Kill Creek wild trout. In addition, together we rambled into a secluded Warner Creek headwater ravine, where I got us lost before Tony found the trail back to our vehicle. We've wandered Garden State trout waters in each other's company and fished many Catskill rivers within sight of one another. Moreover, we constantly swap our Esopus Creek experiences.

So how did such a respected, accomplished individual get the moniker Mr. Spundun? And what the heck is a Spundun anyway?

Well, Tony would be the first person to tell you that he doesn't tie many dry flies using hackle, and luckily for him, he once read the March–April 2003 issue of *American Angler*, a copy of a magazine I also kept. That issue included an Art Scheck article titled "Perpetual Flotation."[1] Scheck's piece introduced a series of patterns the author called "the versatile Spundun," noting that this dry fly is "nearly unsinkable." Hackle is not needed to tie any of these dry flies, only deer hair,

---

[1] Art Scheck, "Perpetual Flotation," *American Angler*, March–April 2003, pp. 52–55.

because the pattern is very similar to a Comparadun-style fly. Scheck credits the idea for his Spundun to Dick Stewart of Dick Surette's Fly Fishing Shop in North Conway, New Hampshire. In the 1970s Stewart created the Skitterbug, tied with deer hair instead of hackle. It was meant to be a hairy alternative to Hewitt's Neversink Skater, because long spade hackle wasn't readily available, while deer hair was easily gotten and floats quite well.

Scheck wrote that "the notion of using hair as dry-fly hackle has always appealed" to him.[2] And, I guess the same was true for Tony Cocozza. Deer hair is readily available and much cheaper than dry-fly necks. Scheck added that he tried tying Skitterbugs himself, but struggled with the process. He experimented "and ended up with a sleek, three-material fly that's practically unsinkable, a cross between Troth Hair Spider and a Comparadun."[3] This was the beginning of a series of dry flies Scheck called the Spundun. The basic Spundun has a tail, dubbed body, and a deer hair wing and thorax. The deer hair wing is spun about the hook shank. Then trimmed beneath the hook and behind the wing, leaving a semicircle of clipped hair for a thorax, and wing on top. Spunduns can be tied in various sizes and shades to represent the numerous mayfly hatches a fly fisher encounters.

This style of dry fly became Tony's favorite, one that he ties in sizes 12 to 16, with an occasional size 18 among them. Tony developed his own Spundun patterns to imitate an *Isonychia*, Light Cahill, March Brown, and Blue-Winged Olive, plus he even developed a tannish-brown pattern for the caddis and other bugs he encounters on Esopus Creek and other Catskill waters. This is Tony's go-to dry-fly pattern, and he often fishes it with a dropper fly a few inches below. It floats well and is a perfect dry fly for the Esopus Creek's foamy pocket waters. Many a fly fisher has sought Tony's Spunduns—he and his flies have become local legends. Though the Spunduns I tie aren't nearly as attractive as Tony's, several size 14 Iso Spunduns are always in my summer fly box,

---

[2] Ibid.
[3] Ibid.

ready to imitate the second brood of Esopus Creek *Isonychia* mayflies that appear in late season, lasting through early autumn.

As Tom Rosenbauer noted, "Finding the right fishing partner is a bit like courting a potential spouse. Hold on to the keepers; they're few and far between."[4] Hail to Tony Cocozza, and long live the Spundun.

Here's my version of an Iso Spundun:

> Hook: Mustad 94840, size 14
>
> Thread: Hot orange, à la Fran Betters
>
> Shuck: Black Z-lon
>
> Body: *Isonychia* (mahogany) beaver dubbing
>
> Wing: Brown deer hair, tied Comparadun style, but spun and clipped behind wing

---

[4] Tom Rosenbauer, "Fishing Buddies," *Anglers Journal*, April 20, 2016, https://www.anglersjournal.com/people/fishing-buddies.

Joe's Caddis

The decade began with the launch of the Hubble Space telescope and start of the Persian Gulf War. The early 1990s also ushered in my introduction to Shenandoah National Park and brook trout fishing the Blue Ridge Mountains with the Jersey Boys. Four of us assembled at Joe David's—aka, Sweetpea—Silver Spring, Maryland home late one Friday in May of 1990. By dawn Saturday, Joe had this magpie group circling the DC beltway and heading southwest toward Front Royal in his blue Dodge Caravan. While Joe drove, John Julian rode shotgun with a map in hand; Little Redneck Rich and I sat in the back seat. Not being one to waste my time, I rummaged through Sweetpea's fly-fishing vest, studying its contents.

The year before, Joe and Rich had made a Yellowstone trip; fished many western rivers while stopping at Blue Ribbon Flies among other places. Though Joe ties some of the best-looking dry flies I've ever seen, he always purchases more at local fly shops whenever traveling. And Joe is a dry-fly man to the core, so that's all he ever purchases.

While I poked through his fly boxes, I stumbled upon a very

interesting caddis pattern, one I had never seen before. So I confiscated it without saying a word. Later, midday while fishing White Oak Canyon Run, I came upon a decent Blue Ridge wild brook trout that rose steadily. Try as I might with several different flies, that fish paid me no mind. So out of pure frustration, I attached the dry I took from Joe's fly box.

On the first cast, that fish took the dry like it was exactly what it had been waiting for, without any hesitation. That would be the last cast I ever made using that fly, because I took it home for a model of future flies. That size 14 dry appeared to have a shuck of dark brown Z-lon, an olive Antron body, and a blonde elk hair downwing clipped off over the hook eye. When I ran into Joe later that day I told him about taking this fly and asked him if he knew its name, to which he replied, "No!" Thus, for many years, we simply referred to this new-found secret pattern as "Joe's Caddis"—Sweetpea's fleeting claim to fame, other than the fact he was once an Olympic high jump athlete.

When I was an active Catskill fly-fishing guide, this dry fly often made the difference between a client catching a trout or not. Years would pass and the success of Joe's Caddis gained piscatorial momentum plus untold fame among the Jersey Boys and other associates. Then one day this balloon burst. I was trolling the internet for trout-fishing information and discovered that dry actually was an X-Caddis, a Craig Mathews pattern from the Blue Ribbon Fly Shop. If I were limited to a single dry-fly pattern for an entire trout season, it would be an olive X-Caddis in sizes 14 to 20. It's that good a trout taker. As for Joe's claim to fame, while attending the University of Maryland, this Terrapin was an Atlantic Coast Conference men's indoor track and field champion three years running, plus a NCAA All-American high jumper the fourth year. So I guess that ain't so bad after all.

Here's my interpreted version of the Craig Mathews X-Caddis:

Hook: Mustad 94840 – size 14 to 20

Thread: Black

Shuck: Brown Z-lon

Body: Orvis no. 66 medium olive Fine & Dry dubbing

Wing: Blonde elk hair, tied downwing

Note, Craig Mathews original X-Caddis pattern called for a deer hair wing and not blonde elk hair like I substituted.

A Dry-Fly Man and the Virtue of Patience

W here do I begin with this narrative? Well, if I'm honest with readers and myself, I begin with a sincere confession and apology. Bless me, Father, for I have sinned—and that I did.

I first encountered Kevan Best while fishing the Esopus Creek more than a decade ago. His exuberance for trout fishing was unmatched, with an appetite for angling knowledge that could fill a bottomless pit, plus his personal warmth should have been contagious. Initially, it overwhelmed me. When we occasionally bumped into each other while fishing the Esopus, Kevan seemed to hang around like a fly stuck to flypaper. He was always friendly and always talkative, sharing his thoughts and zealous love of this pastime, whether I wanted to listen or not. Back then, he might have been somewhat new to fly fishing for trout, full of questions and energetic ideas. To that end, I thought of words from two celebrated anglers, whom some have called patron saints of this sport: Izaak Walton—English author, angler, and early environmentalist, plus John Gierach—noted western author and free-lance writer. In his "Epistle Dedicatory" Walton wrote, "... Angling may be said to be so much like the Mathematicks, that it can ne'r be fully learnt; at least not so fully, but that there will still be more new experiments left for the tryal of other men that succeed us."[1] While John Gierach wrote, "The best fishermen I know try not to make the same mistakes over and over again; instead, they strive to make new and interesting mistakes and to remember what they learned from them."[2] That was Kevan, for sure. Kevan wore his thirst for piscatorial growth and love of this finny pastime on his sleeve while being a totally unassuming and warm, gracious individual.

With the passage of time, I grew a genuine fondness for Kevan—it was hard not to. We belonged to the same Trout Unlimited chapter and that opened my crusty eyes to see him for the fine human being he is. Kevan loves all aspects of fly fishing as much as I do, perhaps more. I grew to know a TU volunteer ready, able, and willing to help others, whether the cause was teaching a youngster how to cast, or planting trees to stabilize stream banks, or just being there when help was needed. He is a thoughtful and giving human being, not to mention an outstanding trout fisher—one of the best dry-fly fishers I ever met. He's also a bamboo fly-rod aficionado with a sweet casting stroke and a true gentleman cut from the cloth of Frederick M. Halford.

Kevan's fly-fishing approach has Halford written all over him. In *Dry-Fly Fishing* Halford wrote, "With the dry or floating fly the angler has in the first instance to find a rising fish, to note accurately the position of, or what is technically called the spot, the rise, and to cast to this fish to the exclusion of any chance work in other parts of the stream."[3] That's Kevan to a tee.

Kevan catches his big trout using dry flies while sight fishing to rising fish, not blind casting with streamers, like me. He waits and watches for trout to rise. On the other hand, I'm a flogger who works at

---

[1] Izaak Walton, *The Compleat Angler* (London: Oxford University Press, 1967), p.7.
[2] John Gierach, *Flyfishing the High Country* (Boulder, CO: Pruett, 1984), p. 5.
[3] Frederick M. Halford, *Dry-Fly Fishing* (Ready, Berkshire: Barry Shurlock, 1973), p. 36.

pounding fish up, and size is never too important to me, as long as the trout are wild fish. I have more of a Brett Favre, gunslinger, chuck-and-chance-it mentality; just get my fly out on the water and see what happens. It was rewarding getting to know him better, even though I may have made it hard at times. So mea culpa. These days we freely swap our trout tales, though our piscatorial appetites might differ a little. I'm lucky to call him a friend.

We both love the Neversink downstream of New York City's reservoir. And while I frequently roam the Esopus Creek watershed, Kevan occasionally graces it with his presence. However, the East Branch of the Delaware River is where we sometimes meet. Kevan pursues selectively feeding brown trout there, as I do occasionally also, but we each have our own favorite spots. In late August 2019, a few months after Kevan retired, he and I twice wandered the East Branch together in a favorite pool of his.

The first time we found this tailwater clear and cold, sometimes with countless Sulfurs drifting by, but only a slim few trout sporadically rose, and those fish were finicky. A bald eagle circled overhead while it rained steadily for a good thirty minutes. Not wishing to waste that time, I tossed a small Black Leech, but never moved a fish, while Kevan waited and watched. Then the rain stopped, and trout started to rise.

I had changed flies so many times, my leader was reduced to a stub. After I lengthened the tippet, a couple of fourteen-to-fifteen-inch browns came my way on a size 20 Blue-Winged Olive Emerger and then a size 20 Once and Away Emerger. Other than nicking one more fish, that was it for me. Kevan, however, persisted, carefully presenting various dry flies over difficult surface-feeding trout. He nicked several fish himself, catching two nice browns, including one beautiful large brown that taped out at the twenty-inch mark.

One week later we fished the same pool together again, only that time Kevan asked me to arrive early to secure our spot, because he would be late. So, I did though that was not my style because we didn't expect trout to start rising until much later in the day. On my own for the first hour, I tossed different streamers through a portion of a cold, sunny pool. Zip, except another angler watched me before departing himself. Thus, I guess I performed my assigned task, holding down the water for the two of us. Later, when I was sitting in one of Kevan's lawn chairs, waiting and watching the river, he arrived.

By then a number of Sulfur duns were floating past us, but rarely did we observe more than a few sporadic rises under the bright sun. In fact, between 1:00 PM and 4:30 PM, we did far more looking, searching, and sitting in lawn chairs than casting flies—not my typical piscatorial modus operandi. I get antsy when not actively engaged, but perhaps now in the later stages of life I'm beginning to learn to slow down. Kevan has worked hard to teach me that approach. As former president Herbert Hoover said, "A fisherman must be of contemplative mind, for it is often long times between bites. Those interregnums emanate patience, reserve, and calm reflection—for no one can catch a fish in anger or in malice."[4]

As Kevan predicted, by 5:00 PM the pool came alive with rising trout in two distinct sizes: big and monsters. After that, for most of the time we fished I kept changing flies, altering my tippet, and scratching my head, saying a few prayers, while Kevan cussed and we both ate large portions of humble pie. I thought for sure I'd be skunked, but I have to tell ya, it *was* exhilarating, casting to those large trout.

While Kevan held down the head of the pool, I picked a pod of big fish at the tailout, worked them hard, and finally experienced a hit—my only hit—to a size 20 Once and Away Emerger on 6X tippet. Kevan netted that trout for me. It measured eighteen inches long, not as big as the brown Kevan caught earlier. That was hard work, graduate-level work, but very rewarding. As the sun dipped over the horizon, the icy-cold East Branch chilled the air, putting a mist over the river, and I got cold, leaving Kevan and the tailwater by 7:30 PM. While driving back home, the warmth of the Tacoma's heater felt good, though it was a late August evening.

On that outing I invested some seven-and-a-half hours on the East

---

[4] Herbert Hoover, *Fishing for Fun and to Wash Your Soul* (New York: Random House, 1963), p. 30-31.

Branch, looking, waiting, sitting, watching, and only fishing less than half that time, with one nice brown to show for a very pleasant day. Kevan touched a couple really nice brown trout before I left him for the evening. And, once again it was grand day spent with a fine dry-fly man.

Sometimes anglers' paths crisscross for a reason and perhaps fishing becomes more about how we catch our trout rather than the fish themselves. Thank you Kevan for being my friend, teaching me to be a better fly fisher, but more importantly the virtue of patience. As lyrics to a 1992 Alabama song go "I'm in a hurry to get things done; Oh, I rush and rush until life's no fun; All I really gotta do is live and die."[5]

---

[5] Alabama, "I'm in a Hurry (and don't know why)," track 10 on *Alabama Greatest Hits, Vol. III*, BMG Music, 1994, compact disc.

Red-Butt Conehead Woolly Bugger

What triggers a trout to strike a fly, anyway? The answers vary. Gary LaFontaine and Gary Borger seemed to agree that trout triggers can be attributed to a fly's size, shape, color, and behavior. In two of his books, *Designing Trout Flies* and *Presentation*, Borger also stressed the role of primary and secondary triggers that can affect selectivity on the trout's part, with one or perhaps more of the triggers the reason why trout take or refuse a fly.

Datus Proper agreed that these are factors, but he placed more emphasis on the fly's behavior as a trigger in *What the Trout Said*. In fact, Proper wrote, "As applied to trout and trout flies, I think nature can be summarized in terms of our list: behavior, size, shape, and color."[1] He dedicated part 2 of this book to behavior, while he set only aside single chapters to cover shape, size, and color. And then there's John Atherton's theory of impressionism expounded in his *The Fly and*

---

[1] Datus Proper, *What the Trout Said: About the Design of Trout Flies and Other Mysteries* (New York: Lyons & Burford, 1989), p. 32.

the Fish. Atherton believed in the "illusion of life," as opposed to exacting imitation, which might not interest a fish at all.

In *Trout Hunting*, Bob Wyatt agrees that "trout are sight feeders, so what we want in a trout fly is a convincing prey-image that incorporates one or more visual triggers,"[2] but he points out that in *Selective Trout*, Doug Swisher and Carl Richards argued that contrary to Atherton's theory, trout are "getting more selective as they are increasingly being fished for, caught, and released," so "the only antidote for this is even more realistic imitation."[3] Wyatt believes that "the natural fly that presents an aspect of vulnerability is doomed to stand out from the herd. This leads to the conclusion that our artificial flies should in fact stand out to some extent from the prevailing food form."[4]

There are lots of ways to make a fly stand out, but one of the most effective is to add a hot spot. Hot spots often are associated with Czech nymphs, though this is debatable, depending upon what one considers a hot spot to be. For instance, did Fran Betters's use of fluorescent orange thread on his Haystack, however small an amount it might have been, constitute a hot spot? Plus, does the yellow egg sack on a classic dry fly such as the Female Beaverkill or the orange post on LaFontaine's Halo Emerger constitute hot spots? Then there are red floss tags on wet flies such as the Governor and Mormon Girl—are they hot spots? And how about the Green Butt Skunk that steelhead respond to?

Plus do hot spots have to be fluorescent or radiate bright colors, or just be contrasting and different? In the Front Range Anglers Fly Shop's blog, I found the following comment, which I fully agree with: "In my opinion, hot spots work by providing an extra stimulus to a fly pattern which sets it apart from the multitude of natural food items (or artificial flies) a fish sees regularly, thereby making it more noticeable, attractive, curious, or any combination of the three."[5] As in so

---

[2] Bob Wyatt, *Trout Hunting: The Pursuit of Happiness* (Mechanicsburg, PA: Stackpole Books, 2005), p. 115.
[3] Ibid, p. 118.
[4] Ibid, p. 116.
[5] Steve McLaughlin, owner, Front Range Anglers, personal communication, February 20, 2022.

many things in fly fishing, the answer is whatever works best in a given situation.

In my pursuit for a better trout fly for winter months, and to bolster my confidence while fishing that late November through early March cold water, I created a Red-Butt Conehead Woolly Bugger, and for that application, a bright color seemed best. A Woolly Bugger just catches trout, especially a small black Bugger, and a cone head gets it down into the trout's zone in cold water, so an additional trigger seemed like a good idea to attract the attention of lethargic trout. Adding a fluorescent red butt to this already successful fly pattern made me confident in tough conditions and trout seem to respond to it.

I can recall two Garden State winter outings when that confidence was put to the test. After my major open-heart surgery, I started cardio rehab in December of 2018 but was still under a list of restrictions when I sweet-talked my wife into letting me fish, a tale I told in a previous chapter. What follows is the second such incident.

January 20th, 2019. The weekend forecast suggested a January thaw and a much-anticipated break in nasty winter weather. Thus, fishing was on my mind. Under a cloudy, damp, forty-degree sky I drove south on I-87. Crossing the state line, I couldn't help but notice the white terrain and ice-capped brooks, which made me wonder what I was doing. Soon, I carefully and slowly trudged down a snow-covered, ice-crusted trail into a concealed ravine and negotiated the hidden footpath like the old man I had grown to be. Fortunately, I wore my studded Vibram wading shoes, so snow would not adhere to their soles. Once at the bottom, I slithered down a steep frozen bank on my butt, and then I rested a good fifteen minutes, because this was a bit of a workout for me. The exercise involved was much different than the cardio rehab I had been engaged in, plus, there wasn't any nurse or instructor watching over me.

The little veiled brook held a good flow, but carried an Adirondack tannic stain and was wintry cold. It was also lined with ice along the creek's edge. It would be a slow journey upstream, and I crashed through snow drifts three times, fortunately always ending upright, but once in cold water up to my knees. Along this slog, I relied upon the services of a size 8 Red-Butt Conehead Woolly Bugger on point with a size 14 Pink Squirrel dropper. My mind was preoccupied with negotiating the terrain, so I wanted help on the fishing end of things, choosing to use two flies that gave me confidence. I fished this duo on a short, tight line, hoping I might catch a single trout. However, I had my doubts because initially my offerings were totally ignored, and I never observed any signs of life except for a scant few midges about.

Well, I did much better than I had any right to expect, though the detected hits caused only the slightest hesitation in my taut leader—hits that came from several different chilly plunge pools, most half covered in ice. Before quitting, I caught four dark, colorful wild rainbows up to ten inches long, all on the Red-Butt Conehead. I didn't push my luck that day, wandering this Garden State winter landscape for not quite two hours.

Less than a month would elapse when I heard the call of the wild again.

February 1st, 2019. My heart surgery was now roughly two-and-half months prior and I was starting to feel like myself once more. The morning was raw, with air temperatures below the freezing mark under a concrete sky of gray-washed clouds. However, the long-term prediction was a Sam Adams' forecast—a cold snap, for beer drinkers—with wind chills below zero and snow on the horizon. Despite snow showers in this day's forecast, I pulled the trigger to fish in search of a February wild trout.

Crossing the state line into New Jersey, I headed back to a favorite Garden State wild-trout brook. The snow was gone from the landscape, but ponds along the drive were still frozen. I trekked down a leaf-covered frozen path into the chilly gorge below. As the air temperature jumped up to the thirty-two-degree mark, I could still see my breath as I moved about. With fingerless fishing gloves on and a latex pair underneath, I again attached my winter rig: a size 8 Red-Butt Conehead Woolly Bugger on point with a size 14 Pink Squirrel dropper.

The brook was icy cold, though I never took the water's temperature.

I use a stream thermometer only during hot summer months to inform me when the water's too warm to fish, but never when it's too cold, because then I don't need an excuse if I never touch a trout during that outing. Besides, most of the plunge pools were almost ice free.

On this outing, I started getting soft hits almost immediately. However, engrossed in fishing I didn't pay attention to where I wandered. As I slithered down a steep, icy bank, I fell down hard and lay on the ground for a bit. More than my ego was bruised. It was a hard fall on my right side. First, I checked my bamboo rod, then I checked myself. All seemed to be OK, but this would come back to haunt me in the weeks to come. As I've noted before, I was on Eliquis—a blood thinner, at the time and bruised badly.

Now, trudging slowly upstream only some four hundred yards, along the way probing plunge pools, deep ice-free pockets, around boulders, over deadfall, loose cobble, and slick fallen leaves, plus the continuous film ice along the creek's edge, I managed to catch seven small wild rainbows up to nine inches long. One trout took the Pink Squirrel, but the other half dozen ate the Red-Butt Conehead Woolly Bugger. I fished for only two hours, because winter snow was on the way. Driving back home, I noticed Department of Transportation crews putting brine down on the roadways, anticipating what was to come.

Some two weeks later, after I got out of a shower one evening, my wife asked me about a major black-and-blue bruise on my right side below my waist, where I fell. My skin was shades of deep purple. I never knew I had this, but it was caused by the tumble in the hollow. I pleaded the Fifth, because some fishing mysteries are best kept secret.

I've relied upon a Red-Butt Conehead Woolly Bugger for several years now. Mostly, I fish it starting in late November through mid-March, when trout waters tend to be cold and often devoid of bug activity. For the most part, I fish it deep, on a dead drift, like a big stonefly nymph, but with a fluorescent red butt; often high-sticking it on a short, tight leader. It works for me.

Red-Butt Conehead Woolly Bugger:

Hook: Mustad 9672, size 8

Head: Small black conehead

Thread: Black

Tail: Short black marabou with four strands of rainbow Krystal Flash

Butt: Fluorescent red chenille

Hackle: Black hackle, palmered

Body: Black chenille

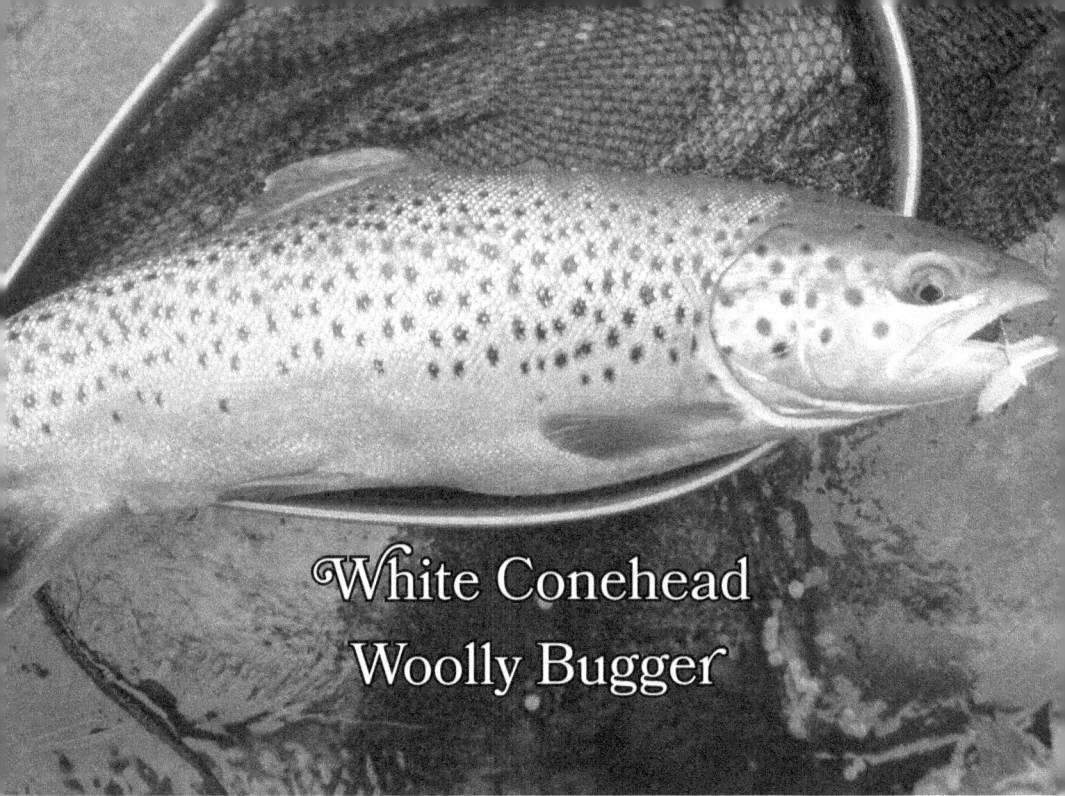

White Conehead Woolly Bugger

'm of the firm belief that white streamers imitate baitfish big reservoir trout are used to foraging on. The late Roger Menard once told me that a white streamer was a favorite choice of his for big autumn brown trout that ran up into Esopus Creek from New York City's Ashokan Reservoir to spawn. What follows is based on an Esopus Creek November 16th, 2014 angling journal entry.

When I left that morning, the stream temperature was four degrees warmer than the air. Esopus Creek measured only forty degrees Fahrenheit, so I wore insulated long johns under my fleece wading pants, plus, I dug out an old pair of neoprene, skin-tight "fat boy" waders. Those old Simms were at least twenty-five years old, maybe older. On that cold outing, the day before my birthday, I could count the number of real days left to fish New York State trout waters in the year on one hand. The end is near, because trout season on Esopus Creek closes two weeks from that day.

Deer hunters were out and about on this second day of their season, while angry, puffy clouds sat atop Catskill peaks, a few still white with snow with another snow event forecast to move in that evening. Upon arrival the Esopus looked forlorn, with a greenish tint, cold and lonely. It's hard to believe another trout season had elapsed. Where are all the fishermen now? And, walking along the banks of the creek I came upon a ten-inch rainbow splashing about near shore. Was it looking to commit suicide or maybe was still attached to a piece of angler's mono-filament? So, I reached down for it and that 'bow quickly disappeared, but I noticed many tiny dark caddis about the rocks. Perhaps that was a good sign. As the day turned out though, I only observed a very few Blue-Winged Olives and just two "once-and-done" rise-forms.

Initially, I fished a size 10 Black Leech with two added BB shot on the tippet, slow and deep. The stream was cold and its bottom slick, as if it wanted to take me down. So, I moved along, as slowly as my Leech. Then it started to snow, which mesmerized me, and I missed a solid strike watching the snow fall instead of my fly line. Missing the hit ticked me off, as this time of year, with a weather front moving in, that could have been costly. It would be the only hit the Leech procured.

I fully intended to pass through this section again, but wondered if my best opportunity already had been spent. Some ten years ago, when I got interested in becoming a serious late-season Esopus streamer fisher, I asked some of the best Esopus fly fishers I knew about this. Their response was always the same: don't expect many fish. A good brown or two an outing is a great day, but Esopus rainbows don't seem to take streamers. Plus, I was told to fish white streamers, most likely to represent the forage baitfish that Ashokan Reservoir spawning-run browns are used to feeding on. However, at the time my favorite late-season streamer colors were yellow and also black. I never really tried white until today, and I'm glad I did.

Retracing my steps, I swung a size 6 White Conehead Woolly Bugger slow and deep. I thought I might have had a couple hits, and soon a seventeen-and-a-half-inch brown confirmed my suspicions. Judging from the trout's fins, it appeared to have been a hatchery fish, but also appeared to have been spawned out. Next, I caught a small, ten-inch wild brown, but then hooked a really good fish.

Waist deep in cold water my feet no longer worked properly, because they were numb. There was no way I could safely find my way back to the bank while playing this trout, so I stood my ground and fought the fish in its own element. It touched my net three times and each time bolted away. Finally, I netted it, with a main goal now of not falling while doing so, not getting wet or losing this prize.

The brown trout turned out to be a twenty-inch female that was dropping fresh eggs. I noticed the eggs on a rock after I quickly released the fish, watching the big brown disappear into the Esopus in a flash. After that, during the last thirty minutes, I never had another hit while I stubbornly continued to fish. When I finally quit, my fingertips and feet stung, telling me it was more than time to stop. Fishing that time of year is not for everyone, just for a few foolish and hardy anglers like me.

It was windy, cold, and spit snow almost the entire time I stood in the icy Esopus that day. On the next day I'd turn sixty-seven years old. One might think I should know better by now. However, that day while I nicked quite a few fallen leaves which floated past me, I also pricked four fish that I was aware of, catching three browns: ten, seventeen-and-a-half, and twenty inches long. It was as good as it gets. As Roderick Haig-Brown wrote in my well-read, worn copy of *A River Never Sleeps*,

> I still don't know why I fish or why other men fish, except we like it and it makes us think and feel. But I do know that if it were not for the strong, quick life of rivers, for their sparkle in the sunshine, for the cold greyness of them under rain and the feel of them about my legs as I set my feet hard down on rocks or sand or gravel, I should fish less often. A river is never quite silent; it can never, of its very nature, be quite still; it is never the same from one day to the next. It has its own life and its own beauty, and the creatures it nourishes are alive and beautiful also. Perhaps fishing is, for me, only an excuse to be near rivers.[1]

---

[1] Roderick Haig-Brown, *A River Never Sleeps* (Toronto: Collins, 1981), p. 352.

Just as Apostle Peter foretold in 1 Peter 4:7–8, the end was near. The Good Lord willing, I'd tie flies and stay plenty occupied in the coming months, but I will miss rivers.

White Conehead Woolly Bugger:

Hook: #6 Mustad 9672

Head: Medium gold conehead

Thread/collar: Hot fluorescent orange

Tail: Short white marabou with four strands of rainbow Krystal Flash

Hackle: palmered white hackle

Body: white chenille over white thread underbody coated with film of head cement

The Wedding Band

In every fly fisher's life, there comes that moment of truth when the angler needs to step up and be accountable, casting your offering in a way and place where your quarry will take it or simply going home unrewarded. Mine came not on a trout stream, but while shopping with my wife.

It was a predictable day that involved my wife, Lois, and me leaving the mountains and driving to Kingston to tackle a lengthy list of errands. Retired folks do that. They bundle their shopping chores, making a single, multipurpose trip into town. On our long to-do list was a quick stop at Kingston Fine Jewelry to fix one of my wife's rings and to address my wedding band.

First things first. Our attendant assisted my wife with her ring while I patiently waited. Now that Lois was satisfied with her results, it was my turn.

I hadn't worn the wedding band in years—no, actually in decades. Initially it was for fear of it falling from my finger disappearing into the depths of a trout stream while I was fishing in cold waters. That sounded all well and good. However, the truth of this matter, and perhaps a somewhat conflicting detail, is that my finger just got too fat and the ring would no longer slide over the knuckle anymore. After the friendly associate behind the store's glass kiosk addressed my wife's needs, she measured my finger so the wedding band could be resized properly. Then she explained the cost of having this done, promptly adding that the value of the wedding band had appreciated to over one thousand dollars in the forty-plus years that we were married. The point the store's employee was trying to make was clearly that the modest charge for this service was well worth the value of its investment.

But I thought, "A thousand dollars, holy mackerel!" Who would have believed that! Should I even be wearing such an expensive ornament?

At that moment, my mind visualized two distinct and different images. One was of my Lois's smiling face once I had the consecrated symbol of our holy bliss resized. And the other was of a new bamboo fly rod that could be acquired from the proceeds of the sale of a ring not worn in decades anyway. What should I do, how should I proceed?

On my part, there was a long, pregnant pause. A tear started to roll down my cheek from a moist eye, while the palm of my left hand sweat and a frog appeared in my throat as two ladies—my wife and the salesperson—patiently waited for the response.

My piscatorial moment of truth had arrived.

"Resize the ring." I responded, revivifying our nuptials at the expense of a new cane rod. After all, what's angling about anyhow, if not capturing the best catch possible?

A Golden Age of Fly Fishing Revisited

Various authors have written about a Golden Age of fly fishing and specifically about the Golden Age of Catskill fly fishing. What was it anyway, and when did it exist? It sounds like something from long ago, perhaps even from an era when wild brook trout dominated Catskill waters, perchance before brown trout caught our fancy. Or maybe it had to do with the use of silk fly lines and cane rods, before spinning rods became popular. Or possibly even swinging a trio of wet flies across and downriver, rather than casting dries tied on chemically sharpened hooks, covered with the latest synthetic high-vis materials. Let's exam a "taste" at what a few authors have written about this mystical time.

The undisputed dean of Catskill fly fishing, Sparse Grey Hackle—also known as Alfred W. Miller—devoted the last chapter of his book *Fishless Days, Angling Nights* to this topic. In it, he wrote, "Golden to me was the decade on the Neversink that ended with 1940. Edward Ringwood Hewitt had some five miles of river. . . his fishing 'camp' was an old farmhouse... Here the 'rods' who rented annual fishing privileges used to assemble at the end of the day for unforgettable nights of fun and companionship and fishing conversation."[1] He went on to add, "And then, while I smoked a pipe and sipped my whisky, he read me the bright narrative which became one of the best chapters in his fascinating autobiography, *Those Were the Days*."[2] Sparse summed it all up by writing

> I can hear his voice yet and see the tackle-littered common room in the lamplight, and I cherish this memory, for the camp is gone now and all that lovely stretch of river where we fished is underneath Neversink Reservoir in sixty feet of water, and Ed long ago crossed that other River to fish from the far bank. That evening was a fragment of the Golden Age, both of the Neversink and of me.[3]

In Alfred Miller's recollection of his Golden Age, there is an association of time, place, incidents, and acquaintances of special import.

William J. Schaldach, in *Currents & Eddies*, painted a colorful picture of the time he spent in the 1920s to the 1930 in the place he called "The Bountiful Beaverkill," when encounters with anglers, trout, and pools filled his days. He lamented that writing about the Beaverkill felt "like a man trying to paint a barn with a water-color brush," concluding, "The Beaverkill is one stream that deserves to live forever—regardless of what may happen in the future."[4]

Dana S. Lamb, a New York City investment banker, fly fisher, author of several fine little angling books, and New York Anglers' Club member, in "Halcyon Days–and Nights" in the Catskills recalled his time at the Antrim Lodge. The Antrim was "where Morgan partners, artists, railroad engineers, sportsmen, bums, ambassadors, industrialists and

---

[1] Sparse Grey Hackle, *Fishless Days, Angling Nights* (New York: Crown, 1971), p. 216

[2] Ibid, p. 222.

[3] Ibid.

[4] William J. Schaldach, *Currents & Eddies* (Rockville Centre, NY: Freshet Press, 1970), pp. 59–60.

politicians of renown wolfed luscious, tender sirloin steaks, drank deep, told lies about their trophies of the angle or the chase and, in the evening, came alive."[5] Who wouldn't wish for these circumstances again?

In "A Modern Proposal for a Speech: The Six Periods of American Flyfishing"[6] in *The American Fly Fisher*, the journal of the American Museum of Fly Fishing, Gordon Wickstrom, a professor of theater and English, author, and avid fly fisher and fly tyer divided the period from 1845 to 2012 into six categories: The Beginning (1845–1900), the Identity Period (1900–1920), the Golden Age (1920–1944), the Transitional Period (1945–1960), the TU Period (1960–2008), and the New Period (2009–2012). His Golden Age of fly fishing was the Golden Age of the Catskills, based with the cane rods, fly tying, tackle, and stories and lore about its people the central themes—all the characteristics of the age that Sparse Grey Hackle, Schaldach, and Lamb recalled so vividly. And, given this background let's take a quick peek at what two noted Catskill angling authors historians wrote.

The late Austin=Mac=Francis was confident enough to title his classic, *Catskill Rivers: Birthplace of American Fly Fishing*. And the birthplace it was with Francis telling the history of the great rivers that flow through this region. In his work he described a certain aura for which he wrote, "Thus the Catskill angling mystique has several attributes that combine the elusiveness of the subtle beauty of the streams, the inner spirit of fully evolved fishermen, and the trout themselves. It manifests itself also in the rare angling companionships that have grown to fruition on these streams."[7]

Along a similar vein, Mike Valla devoted an entire book to dry flies that evolved from this era titled, *Tying Catskill-Style Dry Flies*. In it he wrote, "The history surrounding the development of Catskill style is both long and interesting, and it has led to camaraderie among tiers

---

[5] Dana S. Lamb, "Halcyon Days–and Nights," in *Where the Pools Are Bright and Deep* (New York: Winchester Press, 1973), p. 20.
[6] Gordon Wickstrom, "A Modern Proposal for a Speech: The Six Periods of American Fly Fishing," *American Fly Fisher* 38, no. 3 (Summer 2012), pp. 18–19.
[7] Austin M. Francis, *Catskill Rivers: Birthplace of American Fly Fishing*, (New York: Skyhorse, 2014), p. 5.

who study and practice its tradition. Theodore Gordon, the 'father' of the dry fly in America, certainly had something to do with the evolution and acceptance of the floater in the Catskills and beyond."[8] As further substantiation of this statement, in 1993 Floyd Franke and Matthew Vinciguerra formed the Catskill Fly Tyers Guild. The Guild has been dedicated to preserving, protecting and enhancing the Catskill fly-tying heritage, while promoting the development of future generations of Catskill fly tyers.

In this day of social-media addiction, internet fascination, and online GPS stream coordinates, plus cell phones that never leave one's side, even when fishing, we may have crossed a bridge from such a time that offers no return. Self-discovery is an outdated mode of operation, perhaps with the feel of reading a hardcover book. With Euro nymphing, and fishing-contest fashion the latest rage, a pastime that once pitted man against nature has evolved into a score-keeping event. For some, nature is only as far away as the nearest YouTube video. Crowds of yuppie anglers now sometimes stand where wild trout once swam.

Perhaps we can take refuge in the writing and experience of a long-time western angler. With regard to angling for steelhead, Steve Raymond, a noted fly fisher recently sadly lamented that "today with fewer fish and more fishermen, these quiet periods tend to be longer and more frequent." referring to his own fishless days and angling nights.[9] Yet he added, "a reward for persistence and an affirmation that in lean times, my reason for being on the river is still a valid one . . . because the very next cast may bring a fish that justifies everything."[10] And, "That hope is what keeps me going. As long as I know there is still a chance for success . . . that's enough to fuel my seasonal passion."[11] Thus, despite all the changes in fly fishing in recent times, perhaps a light from the Golden Age can still flicker within us all.

---

[8] Mike Valla, *Tying Catskill-Style Dry Flies*, (Mechanicsburg, PA: Stackpole Books, 2009), pp. 6-9.
[9] Steve Raymond, *A Fly Fisher's Sixty Seasons: True Tales of Angling Adventures*, (New York: Skyhorse, 2018), p. 64.
[10] Ibid, p. 65.
[11] Ibid.

The Last Opening Day

n late 2017, the New York State Department of Environmental Conservation (DEC) held a series of public forums seeking feedback on their existing trout-management plan, which was roughly thirty years old. After various comment periods and several additional public sessions, three years later, in late 2020, the DEC produced a new Trout Stream Management Plan. After that and after more public input, in early 2021, the DEC enacted a new set of trout-stream regulations as a subset of the revised management plan. Basically, these refocused the DEC's management of New York State trout waters on a supporting wild trout while also allowing a year-round catch-and-release period on most trout streams. These regulations had both their supporters and detractors.

What follows is not my position on any of these changes, but merely observations on what some anglers believed was New York's last Opening Day of the trout season. I've participated in Opening Day somewhere for almost sixty years now, and a couple of those years I've been to more than one such event in different states. Thus, if April

1st, 2021 was truly the last New York State Opening Day, as some lamented, it was an affair that I did not want to miss. What follows are pages from my angling log for that day.

April 1st, 2021. Esopus Creek watershed tributaries = Opening Day of trout season, a day much anticipated and a much-loved event, no matter the weather or what river conditions might present. Many stories have been told, some true and some not—jobs affected, health impairments caused, and marriages disrupted. Books such as William Tapply's *Opening Day and Other Neuroses* have been dedicated to the subject. Plus, that book's dust jacket featured a look-alike image of the infamous Saxton Falls on New Jersey's Musconetcong River, an Opening Day scene at its worst, while the word "neuroses" certainly seemed most appropriate. When I was growing up in the Garden State, New Jersey's Opening Days served as a major signal to all those who followed hatchery trucks to get their fishing poles ready.

However, others have written about this event, also—Robert Traver and Nick Lyons, to name but two. Even my lowly penmanship graced covers of prior *Woodstock Times* issues and drew mention in one of the last chapters of my first book. But perhaps the best story I ever read regarding Opening Day was written by my piscatorial hero, Ernest Schwiebert, for the March 28th, 2003, issue of the *New York Times*, titled "Journeys; On Opening Day, a Stream of Memories." in it, Schwiebert harkens back to a time when,

> ... the sport was more like the cloistered rites of some medieval guild. Opening Day of trout season confirmed the ebbing of winter, and its April rituals often seemed a bit like Christmas morning.
>
> People who enjoyed fly-fishing were of the introspective sort, comfortable in their own company, and revered its solitudes. The crosiers and thuribles of their worship were split-cane rods, and reels of precision and elegance, bearing only the tiny hallmarks of their makers. (Garish trademarks emblazoned on fishing tackle still lay in the future.) Our tapered silk lines required

drying overnight and we dressed them at breakfast, using tins of red stag fat from Scotland.

Terminal tackle was Spanish silkworm gut, with the breaking strain of a cobweb in its thinnest diameters. Dry gut was brittle and frail, and required careful wetting between felt pads moistened with glycerin and distilled water. Fishing vests and bug spray did not exist. Old-timers used citronella, and even memories of its smell evoke a thousand echoes. British fly boxes had transparent spring-loaded lids on each compartment, and clips for wet flies, filled with the magic of artisans who worked in fur, feathers and steel.

There were English pipes and the smell of expensive tobacco, and the anglers we knew were knowledgeable about wines and spirits, and the pleasures of good cookery.

Most wore rumpled jackets of worn barleycorn Shetland, frayed herringbones from the Cheviot Hills and subtle tweeds from the thatch-roofed crofter's cottages of Connemara, Ireland. Many insisted on wearing neckties, because trout were gentlemen, and one dressed like a gentleman to enjoy the privilege of fishing.[1]

But times have changed, and this was the last Opening Day. What follows is my account of April 1st, 2021.

Wind howled all night, and rain fell clanking through downspouts. I was up at first light and checked the USGS gage for Neversink flows downstream of New York City's dam. The river is on the rise again, with rain and snow in today's forecast, crushing all sensible hope of fishing that tailwater. Many Catskill waters came up overnight again; the Esopus was a raging muddy mess. But after all, it is Opening Day. As I packed my Tacoma, sleet bounced off the truck-bed tonneau cover. Then, as I was driving north on NY 28, wet snowflakes splattered

---

[1] Ernest Schwiebert, "Journeys; On Opening Day, a Stream of Memories," *New York Times*, March 28, 2003, https://www.nytimes.com/2003/03/28/travel/journeys-on-opening-day-a-stream-of-memories.html.

against the windshield. This was a classic Catskill Opening Day. So today, I would utilize two old-time Opening Day favorites, two weighted nymphs: a size 12 Epeorus on point with a size 14 Hare's Ear dropper some eighteen inches above it. And I initially fished a small Catskill hollow located in the headwaters of Bush Kill Creek, not far from Peekamoose, the kind of place some folks write about. T. Morris Longstreth did in his 1918 classic, *The Catskills*.

The tiny brook held a good flow, was clear, but thirty-seven-degrees cold. Life seemed nonexistent in this winterlike setting, except for the two small wild brook trout I caught and a third one I spooked. During this trek, various fingertips went numb, though I wore latex and fleece fingerless fishing gloves. Plus, this terrain seems to have grown steeper, the water colder, and the trout harder to catch after so many Opening Days have now come and gone. Nevertheless, these things are to be expected on Opening Day, especially with the passage of time. About the only thing physically left of my angling past is the youthful exuberance for the trout I still pursue.

Having wandered as much as I could have there, I relocated to the upper end of another Catskill hollow, Traver Hollow, at a dirt road terminus. Initially, I fished The Vertical, a series of steep, full-bodied plunge pools that flank Samuels Point, catching two small browns, one of them a colorful, plump trout of some nine inches. Then I explored a tiny branch that drains New York State Forest Preserve lands on Cross Mountain/Mount Pleasant. This flow is so small that typically I wander the tiny trib only in early April. In doing so today, I picked up two more small wild browns.

Finally, I relocated one last time, downstream a tad on Traver Hollow, hoping to seduce a spawning rainbow that might have run upstream and out of New York City's Ashokan Reservoir in search of gravel in which to drop eggs. However, I never detected a single hit in the foamy, healthy, cold whitewater flow, but I did notice fresh wet boot prints on streamside rocks. Then I encountered a neighbor, who had already bait-fished this section, yet never experienced a hit, either, so I quit fishing at 1:30 PM.

Thus, the 2021 New York State Opening Day was in the books. I flogged two different Esopus Creek watershed tributaries for a few hours, sometimes with snow falling, catching six small wild trout, five to nine inches long: four browns and two brookies. Four of these ate the Epeorus Nymph, while two preferred the Hare's Ear dropper while I was high sticking the flies on a short, tight leader. Each hit was not much more than a light love tap in the cold Catskill water.

So, if today was the last official New York State Opening Day, let the piscatorial record books show that I participated despite nasty weather and high, cold flows. But Schwiebert is right: Opening Day is a ritual for fly fishers, and it will endure whether the State of New York recognizes it or not. So come April 1st, 2022, the Good Lord willing, I hope my wife will do all those traditional Opening Day things again: make me a French toast breakfast, pack a fried-egg sandwich for lunch—really messing with my daily cholesterol—and provide a thermos of hot coffee while I put on my official Opening Day hat. Some traditions never die, nor can they be regulated away.

Over the decades, I have taken part in this ceremony on streams in New Jersey, New York, and Pennsylvania. Each one was unique and special. But to that end, allow me to quote myself once again with an often-used verse from "Rituals, the First Day and the Last" of my first book: "So perhaps many of us are creatures of habit, followers of rituals. The opening and last day of each trout season are just part of the fabric of our lives. And I guess it's all the other outings between these bookend rituals that can become commonplace, lost in the fragments and dark places of our angling minds if allowed to happen; but these two days are clearly special."[2]

To all those who grieve the loss of New York State Opening Days, keep the faith while enjoying and remembering every day between your first and last trout outing of this year and every one yet to come.

---

[2] Ed Ostapczuk, *Ramblings of a Charmed Circle Flyfisher* (Bloomington, IN: Xlibris, 2012), p. 178.

Epilog

The first draft of this tome was completed almost a year ago, on April 1st, 2021—Opening Day of New York's trout season. Then it went into edit mode for several months as my trout season unfolded. In late 2021 as I begun a final review of edited notes, we learned my wife had cancer, and our lives changed on a dime.

Though I fished, and caught a few trout in December of 2021 bringing that pursuit to one-hundred-seventeen consecutive months, interest in trying to catch a trout on a fly each consecutive month was gone. It seemed like a silly, worthless exercise, even though I truly enjoyed fly fishing for trout every month of the year, pitting myself against nature. In January of 2022 I didn't fish, giving my undivided attention to my wife. Then the only streak that mattered was continuing to see her smiling face every day.

As for fishing, it's clearer to me now than ever before, make every cast count, enjoy every trout encountered to the max. As René Harrop skillfully noted in *Trout Hunter*, "Treat each trout as an individual and with respect. A wild trout is a worthy opponent; therefore, study it carefully and take nothing for granted."[1] Words to pursue this pastime and angle by.

February 2022

---

[1] Harrop, René, *Trout Hunter: The Way of an Angler*, (Boulder, CO: Pruett Publishing Company, 2003), p. 8.

About the Author

Ed resides in Shokan, New York with his wife Lois; both are retired. They have four grown children and ten grandchildren. He spent half his working years employed by the IBM Corporation and the other half teaching mathematics in New York's public school system. Other than family, his passion is trout fishing which he began at an early age and has been flyfishing for Catskill trout since the late 1960s. And he is lucky enough to fish over one-hundred-fifty days most years with the majority of this time spent on two watersheds that drain Slide Mountain: Esopus Creek and the Neversink.

In 1969 as a junior in college he joined Trout Unlimited and has been a continuous member of that organization since. Currently he is involved in the Ashokan-Pepacton Watershed Chapter of Trout Unlimited, as well as maintaining memberships in other regional organizations.

Given years of involvement with trout stream conservation, he received several local, regional, and national recognitions for these activities including the Salmo Award from Theodore Gordon Flyfishers in 1981 and Trout Unlimited National's Trout Conservation Award in 1982. In April of 2018 the Catskill Fly Fishing Center & Museum recognized Ed as a Catskill Legend. He has several published articles on education and trout fishing, writes a standing column for the Catskill Fly Tyers Guild newsletter, and in 2012 published the book *Ramblings of a Charmed Circle Flyfisher*.

www.ingramcontent.com/pod-product-compliance
Lightning Source LLC
Chambersburg PA
CBHW031202270326
41931CB00006B/373